AF693602

How to Write and Self-Publish Podcasts - Using AI

How to Write and Self-Publish Podcasts - Using AI

Dakota Frandsen

First Printing, 2026

CONTENTS

The world of podcasting is a dynamic, evolving space where creators share unique stories, knowledge, and perspectives. While ingenuity and passion have always been at its core, a new, transformative force is now emerging: **artificial intelligence (AI)**. This book is founded on the belief that AI is not just a tool but a powerful ally, capable of amplifying creativity, streamlining workflows, and unlocking unprecedented production quality and audience engagement for podcasters.

We are living in an era of exciting opportunity. The barriers to creating high-quality audio content are lower than ever, yet the challenge of achieving visibility in a crowded market has grown. AI provides a potent solution, helping new creators overcome technical obstacles and freeing established podcasters to focus on their message and their audience. From generating innovative episode concepts and crafting compelling scripts to surgically polishing audio and creating custom soundtracks, AI is fundamentally changing every stage of the podcasting journey.Why This Guide Is Essential Now

Podcasting thrives on intimacy, authenticity, and the human voice, offering a personal connection that transcends other digital media. However, as the landscape becomes more competitive, creators face the dual challenge of consistently producing high-quality content and finding innovative ways to engage their target audience. This is precisely where the synergy between podcasting and AI creates an exciting new frontier.

AI, now an accessible reality, is permeating every industry, and content creation is no exception. For podcasters, AI is an **opportunity to amplify creativity**, not a threat to it. Imagine an AI that can:

- Uncover your next viral episode idea from vast data sets.
- Instantly polish your audio to a professional standard.

- Generate unique background music perfectly tailored to your show's mood.

These are the current capabilities that can fundamentally transform your production workflow.What This Book Offers

This guide is meticulously designed for the modern podcaster—whether you are just launching your show or are a seasoned professional seeking a technological edge. Our goal is to demystify AI, presenting it as a practical, accessible toolkit rather than an intimidating frontier.

This book serves as your essential roadmap to navigating this transformative intersection. We will provide clear explanations, actionable advice, and relevant examples to empower you to:

- **Elevate your content:** Use AI for initial concept development and sophisticated scriptwriting.
- **Enhance your efficiency:** Apply AI to recording, editing, music creation, and cover art design.
- **Deepen your connection:** Leverage AI for sophisticated audience analysis and engagement.

Prepare to embark on a journey that will redefine your understanding of what is possible, ensuring you not only keep pace with innovation but lead the charge in the next generation of audio storytelling.

1

The Dawn of Podcasting and the AI Revolution

The world of audio content creation has experienced a dramatic shift, transforming podcasting from a niche pursuit into a global phenomenon that fundamentally alters how people consume media and information. This explosive growth signals the democratization of content creation, significantly lowering the barriers to entry and fostering an unprecedented diversity of voices, experiences, and expertise.

However, this accessibility presents a new challenge: standing out in a crowded marketplace. With millions of podcasts vying for attention, creators must be strategic, efficient, and relentlessly focused on high quality. Listeners have developed a discerning ear, demanding well-researched, clearly produced, and consistently delivered content. This demanding environment is precisely where Artificial Intelligence (AI) emerges not just as a useful tool, but as a strategic necessity.AI: The Podcaster's Strategic Imperative

AI is rapidly offering tangible, practical solutions that elevate production value, streamline workflows, and enhance impact. It can automate repetitive tasks, assist with research and scriptwriting, analyze data, and even aid in technical audio production, providing a significant competitive advantage for both new and established creators.

The potential of AI is immense. Imagine an AI sifting through historical documents for obscure facts, generating multiple interview question variations, analyzing audience feedback for subtle preferences, or creating custom background music. These are not future fantasies but increasingly common realities for creators who embrace this technology.

This guide is designed to demystify AI, breaking down complex concepts and demonstrating how AI can be your co-pilot throughout the entire podcasting journey—from the initial idea to the final polished episode.Demystifying AI: Practical Tools for Creators

AI, often mistakenly associated with complex algorithms and futuristic robots, is an accessible and indispensable ally for the modern podcaster. Think of AI as an intelligent, tireless assistant and sophisticated editor that augments human capability.

At its core, AI refers to computer systems performing tasks that typically require human intelligence, such as understanding language (Natural Language Processing or NLP) and learning from data (Machine Learning or ML).

Machine Learning (ML) teaches computers to learn from vast datasets, allowing AI to perform tasks like predicting listener engagement, suggesting optimal episode release times based on audience behavior, or recommending script flow improvements. It acts as a hyper-observant apprentice with comprehensive knowledge of the podcasting landscape.

Natural Language Processing (NLP) enables computers to understand, interpret, and generate human language. This is where AI truly shines for content creators:

- **Accelerated Research:** NLP allows AI to process the huge volume of text involved in podcasting—transcripts, research papers, articles, and feedback. For instance, an AI can sift through hundreds of documents, extract key themes, identify relevant quotes, and generate concise summaries in minutes, dramatically accelerating the research phase.
- **Script Refinement and Brainstorming:** AI tools can assist with writer's block by generating draft paragraphs, suggesting phrasing, or brainstorming talking points from a few keywords or a basic outline. The AI provides a foundation that the creator can then refine and infuse with their unique voice.
- **Transcription and Summarization:** AI-powered transcription is becoming incredibly accurate and efficient, saving hours of manual typing. Furthermore, AI can take a transcript and generate a concise summary for show notes, social media posts, or content review.

Revolutionizing Production and Audience Engagement

AI's utility extends significantly into the production and post-production phases:

- **Audio Editing Efficiency:** While not replacing the nuanced human ear, AI can automate repetitive tasks like identifying and removing filler words ("um," "uh") or long pauses, improving pacing and listenability. It can also help with intelligent noise reduction and level optimization, freeing the creator to focus on storytelling.
- **Problem-Solving and Creative Augmentation:** AI acts as a super-powered research assistant, accelerating information gathering for complex topics. For interview-based shows, it can analyze an interviewee's past work to suggest informed, insightful follow-up questions, moving the dialogue beyond the superficial.

For scripted content, AI serves as a brainstorming partner, generating scenarios or plot twists that spark human creativity.

- **Data-Driven Content Strategy:** AI analyzes listener data (downloads, retention rates, engagement patterns) to identify hidden trends. An AI could pinpoint segments that cause listener drop-off or topics that correlate with higher engagement, allowing podcasters to make informed, strategic decisions about content structure, topics, and marketing efforts.

The Ethical Compass: Authenticity and Transparency

The rapid integration of AI requires a strong moral compass to navigate ethical implications, ensuring innovation does not compromise responsible practice.

- **Authenticity and Disclosure:** Podcasting relies on the host's genuine voice. When AI is used for scriptwriting, voice synthesis, or content generation, the line between human and machine output can blur. Creators must maintain authenticity through transparency, clearly disclosing the extent of AI involvement. This is crucial for maintaining audience trust, especially in genres relying on personal narrative or human vulnerability.
- **Impact on Human Creativity:** Over-reliance on AI could stifle original thought and devalue the skill of human creators. The ethical challenge is to balance AI as a tool to *enhance* human capabilities (overcoming blocks, exploring possibilities) rather than *replace* them. The human creator must remain the strategic director, ensuring the podcast's soul is driven by human intuition and artistic vision.
- **Intellectual Property and Bias:** AI models trained on vast datasets risk inadvertently infringing on copyright or perpetuating biases present in the training data (e.g., gender, race). Podcasters must critically evaluate AI-generated content for originality

and ensure it aligns with principles of fairness and inclusivity, actively fact-checking and mitigating any harmful prejudices.

The Future of AI-Assisted Podcasting

The future promises even more sophisticated AI capabilities:

- **Hyper-Personalized Content:** AI may dynamically adjust episode pacing, emphasize specific segments, or generate personalized intros based on a listener's individual preferences. The ethical imperative here is to ensure AI fosters intellectual curiosity and exposes listeners to diverse perspectives, rather than creating detrimental filter bubbles.
- **Advanced Autonomy:** AI will likely be able to autonomously generate entire, polished podcast episodes from prompts, complete with realistic synthesized voices and sound design. This underscores the need for greater transparency, and the human role will evolve to that of curator and strategic guide.
- **Enhanced Discovery and Engagement:** AI will further refine audience-matching algorithms, leading to more efficient discovery. It could also power interactive experiences, such as AI-driven chatbots answering listener questions or facilitating community discussions, deepening the creator-audience connection.

By embracing continuous learning, focusing on uniquely human skills like emotional intelligence and storytelling, and maintaining a strong ethical framework of transparency and responsibility, podcasters can confidently navigate the AI revolution. The future of podcasting is a powerful partnership between human ingenuity and artificial intelligence, offering unparalleled opportunities to innovate, connect, and thrive.

2

Laying the Foundation - Your Podcast's Identity

Before recording a single word, the most critical step for any podcast is defining its core identity: **What is your podcast *for*?** In a crowded audio landscape, merely having a topic is insufficient. You must articulate your unique value proposition, clearly identifying *who* you are speaking to, *why* they should listen, and *how* your voice will stand out. This foundational work—defining your niche and purpose—is the bedrock of a successful audio endeavor.

The journey begins with introspection. Identify the topics that genuinely ignite your passion, the subjects you could discuss endlessly. This enthusiasm is infectious and captivating.

- **Follow Your Passion:** Think about the subjects you *love* and are deeply invested in, whether it's historical minutiae, niche scientific fields, or a particular hobby. Your genuine curiosity, much like that of the hosts of "Reply All" when exploring the internet's eccentricities, will draw listeners in.
- **Pair Passion with Research:** Enthusiasm alone is not enough; you need an audience. Conduct research to understand potential listeners' needs, pain points, curiosities, and existing content consumption. Tools like Google Trends, Reddit, and keyword research provide invaluable insights. For example, ex-

ploring a "zero-waste" community on Reddit can reveal the challenges and information gaps of potential listeners, moving your focus from a vague interest to a specific audience segment.

- **Narrow Your Focus:** The key to traction is specificity. Broad topics like "Business" are too vague. Niche down: "Small business marketing" is better; **"Marketing for independent bookstores" is a specific, go-to resource niche.** This specificity, exemplified by "The Allusionist's" deep dive into word etymology, makes your podcast indispensable to the *right* audience, rather than merely available to a broad one.

Beyond the "what" (the niche), you must define the "why"—the fundamental purpose that guides all content and marketing decisions.

- **To Educate:** The goal is to impart knowledge clearly. Content is fact-driven, well-researched, and structured to demystify subjects, like "Stuff You Should Know" explaining everyday topics.
- **To Entertain:** The focus is on compelling narratives, humor, captivating personalities, or storytelling. Shows like "Conan O'Brien Needs a Friend" rely on the host's charisma and engaging conversation to provide laughter and escapism.
- **To Build Community:** The aim is to foster a sense of belonging and shared identity. This involves interactive segments, listener call-ins, and creating a hub for like-minded individuals, common among fandom or professional groups.
- **Intentional Design:** Your purpose must be intentional. Don't *hope* to entertain; *design* your content to entertain. Don't *hope* listeners learn; *structure* your content to educate. This clarity informs every production and marketing choice.

Once you have a niche and a purpose, you must validate the concept and articulate what makes your show unique.

- **Validate Demand:** Test your concept in a low-stakes way. Talk to potential listeners, run informal surveys, or engage in online forums. Observing what topics generate the most discussion provides invaluable feedback for refinement. Analyze successful shows in your niche to identify gaps, such as how "Maintenance Phase" filled the need for debunking health and wellness pseudoscience with critical thinking.
- **Establish Your Unique Selling Proposition (USP):** Your USP is the answer to: "Why *my* podcast over all the others?" It's the core differentiator—the secret sauce that makes your show irresistible.

    - **Unique Format/Structure:** The way you present content (e.g., exclusively unsolved true crime, themed narrative arcs like *This American Life*).
    - **Distinctive Perspective/Angle:** *How* you look at the subject matter (e.g., financial advice only for artists, current events analyzed through a historical lens).
    - **Niche Expertise/Authority:** Leveraging deep, specialized knowledge (e.g., an archaeologist hosting a podcast on ancient Roman plumbing).
    - **Unique Interaction/Community:** Actively involving listeners and fostering a strong sense of community (e.g., extensive listener Q&A, the unique host dynamic of *SmartLess*).
    - **Unconventional Tone/Personality:** The host's personality and the overall feel (e.g., blending rigorous science with irreverent humor like *This Podcast Will Kill You*).
- **The Iterative Process:** Defining your niche and purpose is an ongoing evolution. Be prepared to adapt and refine your focus based on audience feedback and the dynamic landscape of your show.

To create truly resonant content, you must move beyond vague generalizations and craft a detailed profile of your ideal listener—the **Listener Avatar**.

- **Demographics (The Who):** Statistical data: age, gender, location, income, occupation. (e.g., Individuals aged 25-40, part-time working parents, $90k household income).
- **Psychographics (The Why):** Inner world data: values, beliefs, attitudes, motivations, pain points, aspirations. (e.g., Anxious about parenting ability, seeks evidence-based but relatable advice, values authenticity, feels isolated).
- **Research Methods:**

    - **Surveys:** Mix quantitative (rating scales) and qualitative (open-ended questions like "What is your biggest challenge right now?") to gather data on preferences and pain points.
    - **Online Communities:** Immerse yourself in platforms like Reddit and specialized forums to observe the language, common questions, and emotional undercurrents of your audience.
- **Flesh Out the Avatar:** Give your persona a name (e.g., "Stressed but Hopeful Sarah") and a detailed backstory. This tangible person becomes your compass during content planning, ensuring every episode is relevant, engaging, and addresses their specific needs.

Your name, tagline, tone, and voice are the ambassadors that ensure your podcast is both **discoverable and magnetic**.

Your name is the first handshake; your tagline is the elevator pitch that communicates your core value proposition.

- **Clarity Over Cleverness:** While a name can be clever (like *Freakonomics Radio*), it must offer a strong clue about the content.
- **Incorporate Keywords:** Use terms potential listeners would search for (e.g., "Victorian Mysteries: Unsolved Crimes of the 19th Century").
- **Tagline as Value Proposition:** The tagline answers: "Why should I listen?" It must be concise, descriptive, and benefit-driven.

    - **Example (Name: *Concrete Roots*):** Tagline: "Urban gardening made simple for apartment dwellers."
- **Check Availability:** Crucially, verify the name on major podcast directories, social media handles, and for domain names to ensure brand consistency and avoid legal issues.

Tone is the attitude; voice is the expression. They are the personality that transforms listeners into loyal followers.

- **Tone is Attitude:** Is it conversational (like friends over coffee, e.g., *My Brother, My Brother and Me*), formal (authoritative and structured, e.g., *Serial*), humorous (*Sawbones* blending wit with education), or inspirational?
- **Voice is Delivery:** Cadence, vocabulary, use of humor/gravitas, and pacing. Enthusiasm and sincerity are infectious.
- **Consistency is Key:** Maintain your established personality across all episodes and all aspects of presentation (scripting, delivery, music selection) to avoid jarring or confusing your audience.
- **Alignment:** Your tone must align with your niche, purpose, and ideal listener. For example, personal finance for young adults is best served by a relatable, encouraging tone, while complex science requires an authoritative, clear voice.

This intentional, deliberate approach to defining your niche, purpose, audience, and brand identity is the difference between shouting into the void and having a meaningful conversation with an audience eager to listen. It is the solid foundation for building a sustainable, impactful, and memorable podcast.

3

Essential Gear for the Modern Podcaster

A truly professional podcast is not solely defined by the choice of a flagship microphone or a powerful Digital Audio Workstation (DAW); it is a meticulously crafted sound experience built upon the foundation of high-quality accessories and a perfectly tuned acoustic environment. These "finishing touches" are, in reality, indispensable components that transform raw vocal capture into the clear, present, and professional audio demanded by today's listeners. By controlling the sound *before* it becomes data, podcasters minimize post-production effort and maximize sonic clarity.

Essential Tools for Pristine Vocal Capture

The microphone is the sensor, but its critical accessories act as environmental controls, ensuring that only the desired audio reaches the diaphragm, free from jarring mechanical or breath-related artifacts.

Accessory	**In-Depth Function and Rationale**	**Profession[al] and Selection**

Pop Filter (Pop Shield)	This crucial barrier is designed to disrupt and diffuse the sudden burst of air pressure created by plosive consonants, primarily "P"s, "B"s, and sometimes "T"s and "K"s. Without diffusion, this air stream slams into the microphone's sensitive capsule, causing a low-frequency, overwhelming "pop" or "thump."	**Selection:** Cl mesh fabric scree fective and often thin metal screen clean and offer m frequency attenu **ment:** Position th inches away from the speaker 2–4 i from the filter, cr tinct zones of pro
Shock Mount	Sound waves are transmitted not only through the air but also through solid objects (structure-borne noise). A shock mount is an elastic suspension system—often consisting of internal bands or an external web of elastic cords—that cradles the microphone. Its sole purpose is to acoustically and physically isolate the mic from vibrations that travel up the stand from desk bumps, foot traffic, heavy keyboard typing, or external rumbling from traffic.	**Benefit:** Elim tically reduces lov rumbles, hums, a that are notoriou remove without c the voice's natura cies in post-produ Most high-end cc ribbon micropho custom-fit shock timal performanc

Microphone Stand/Boom Arm	Stability and precise, repeatable positioning are paramount for consistency in episode-to-episode recording. The stand elevates the mic off the work surface, dramatically reducing the transmission of desk-related vibrations. Boom arms, in particular, offer superior flexibility.	**Selection: Bo** highly recommen allow for easy, qu ing, free up desk keep the microph the speaker's mou the *Proximity Ef* **Stands** with heav offer stability for or large mic setu **sideration:** Ensu weight capacity c weight of your m shock mount.
Cables (XLR, USB)	The cable is the essential conduit for the audio signal. For professional-grade microphones (dynamic and condenser), **XLR cables** are the standard. They utilize a *balanced* three-pin configuration that effectively rejects Electromagnetic Interference (EMI) and Radio Frequency Interference (RFI) over long distances, preserving a clean signal.	**Quality Mat** standard cable tr high-quality cabl bust shielding (b and durable conn venting intermitt and noise ingress **Microphones:** C quality, shielded an appropriate le mize data dropo cal noise.

The Critical Imperative of Acoustic Control

A recording studio is not merely a quiet space; it is a *controlled* acoustic environment. A pristine microphone will faithfully capture the sound of a poor room, resulting in audio that sounds hollow, echoey, or "boxy"—a sound quality that screams amateur. The goal of acoustic treatment is to manage the sound waves *after* they leave the speaker's mouth but *before* they return to the microphone as unwanted reflections.

Acoustic Solution	**Detailed Mechanism and Placement Strategy**	**Impact on Fi Quality**
Acoustic Absorption	These materials—often open-cell foam, fiberglass, or mineral wool—are designed to *absorb* sound energy, converting it into trace amounts of heat. They prevent sound waves from reflecting back to the microphone.	**Placement:** F **Primary Reflect Points**—the wall desk surfaces whe bounces first. A k placing absorptio hind the speaker (flections from the the mic) and on t faces immediately the microphone.
Soft Furnishings & Improvised Treatment	Before investing in specialized panels, leverage the natural absorption properties of soft household items. Heavy velvet or blackout curtains, plush rugs over hard floors, upholstered furniture, and bookshelves filled with irregularly shaped objects all help to dampen high and mid-frequency reflections.	**Cost-Effectiv** The classic "recor closet full of cloth highly effective be ing acts as exceller provised absorpti dramatically mini reflections for im clarity.

Diffusion	Unlike absorption, diffusion works by *scattering* sound energy rather than eliminating it. Diffusers feature irregular, non-symmetrical surfaces (e.g., QRD diffusers) that break up the energy of sound waves and redistribute them across the room at different angles.	**Benefit:** Esse studios, diffusior room's liveliness preventing stand flutter echo. It m sound bigger anc avoiding the "dea overly absorbed
Reflection Filter (Vocal Shield)	This is a portable, curved acoustic baffle that mounts directly to the mic stand, encircling the back and sides of the microphone. It's an effective solution for podcasters in untreated spaces.	**Function:** It highly absorptiv ble immediately the microphone. blocks reflection noise attempting mic from behind capturing a drier vocal track.

Mastering the Acoustic Sweet Spot and Room Dynamics

Achieving superior audio quality is often less about the gear and more about intelligent positioning within your recording space.

1. **Avoid Immediate Reflections:** Never record with the microphone pointed directly at a large, bare surface like a window, a large painting, or a flat wall. The sound will bounce back almost instantly, causing **comb filtering**, which manifests as a hollow or thin quality in the voice.
2. **Minimize Low-Frequency Build-up (Room Modes):** Low-frequency sound waves (bass) are long and powerful. In rectangular rooms, they often stack up in corners and along walls,

creating **standing waves** or **room modes** that cause an exaggerated, muddy bass response in specific locations. Avoid placing your mic or speaker system directly in a corner. For rooms with severe bass issues, professional **Bass Traps** (thick, dense absorbers designed for corners) are the only true solution.

3. **Proximity Effect for Voice:** Leverage the **Proximity Effect**—the natural increase in bass frequencies that occurs when using directional (cardioid) microphones close to the source. Positioning the microphone a few inches from your mouth adds desirable warmth and richness to the voice, helping it cut through the mix.
4. **The Test, Listen, Move Cycle:** No amount of theoretical knowledge replaces critical listening. Record a 30-second test phrase, listen back on quality headphones, then slightly adjust your mic angle or your seating position, and record again. Aim for the position that yields the most direct, warm, and reflection-free sound.

By meticulously attending to both the accessories that condition the signal and the environment that shapes the sound, you establish a professional acoustic foundation. This approach dramatically reduces the need for heavy-handed digital manipulation, allowing your voice to sound natural, compelling, and utterly professional.

4

AI-Powered Content Ideation and Planning

The landscape of content production, particularly in podcasting, has been fundamentally transformed by the integration of Artificial Intelligence (AI). Far from merely being a utility, AI-powered tools function as a sophisticated, always-on partner at every stage of the podcast lifecycle. This collaboration turns the often-daunting, time-consuming task of content generation, research, and promotion into a strategic, highly data-driven, and supremely efficient workflow, enabling creators to focus on the unique creative value they bring.

1. AI-Driven Topic Ideation: Silencing the Blank Page and Predicting Success

The notorious anxiety of "what to talk about next" is now replaced by a proactive, data-driven wellspring of inspiration. AI doesn't guess; it uses complex pattern recognition to guide content strategy toward proven audience interest and emerging trends.

- **Analyzing Real-Time Data for Predictive Relevance:** AI systems constantly sift through vast, disparate data streams—including trending search queries, volatile social media discussions, long-form articles, and peer-reviewed academic research. This continuous analysis identifies intricate patterns and nascent movements (e.g., the rising prominence of the *circular economy in fashion*, the logistical challenges of *biodegradable packaging* implementation), allowing podcasters to pivot toward relevance before topics reach peak saturation.

- **Deep Understanding of Audience Sentiment and Intent:** Beyond simple keyword counting, AI excels at Natural Language Processing (NLP) to gauge the emotional core of audience discussions. By analyzing comments, forum threads, and social media replies, it identifies specific, acute pain points (such as the widespread frustration of *managing student loan debt post-pandemic* or the intricacies of work-life balance in remote settings). This capability moves content development from generic themes to highly specific, empathetic solutions.
- **Identifying Emerging Sub-Niches and Establishing Authority:** The goal in a saturated market is not to be louder, but to be more specific. AI acts as a finely tuned radar, detecting nascent areas of interest within broad fields. For example, it might suggest exploring *ethical considerations in AI-powered hiring processes* rather than tackling a general discussion on AI. By helping podcasters stake a claim in these micro-niches, AI facilitates their rapid ascent to subject matter authority.
- **Uncovering Overlooked Narratives and Unique Angles:** AI cross-references existing popular content to detect areas where the mainstream narrative is incomplete or superficial. This analysis highlights overlooked perspectives or under-explored arguments on otherwise popular subjects. For instance, instead of focusing on the major battles of WWII, AI might suggest an episode discussing *civilian life in occupied territories* during the conflict, guaranteeing a fresh, compelling perspective.
- **Proactive Competitor and Content Gap Analysis:** AI can systematically audit competitors' content libraries and performance metrics. It precisely pinpoints areas where competitors are

not focusing, where their coverage is superficial, or where their audience is signaling unmet curiosity. This intelligence is crucial for developing a unique selling proposition (USP) and offering a deeper, more valuable dive that attracts and retains listeners.

2. AI as a Research Accelerator: Ensuring Accuracy, Depth, and Credibility

The foundation of compelling content is rigorous research. AI significantly streamlines the move from initial topic selection to a well-informed, evidence-based episode, radically compressing the time spent on information gathering and verification.

- **Intelligent Information Summarization and Distillation:** AI tools ingest and process overwhelming volumes of text, such as 50-page academic papers, lengthy government reports, or complex legal documents. They rapidly provide concise summaries that distill core arguments, key findings, and methodologies, offering a high-level overview in minutes rather than hours.
- **Precision Key Information Extraction (KIE):** Rather than reading for hours to find a single fact, AI can be directed to precisely target and extract specific data points, verifiable statistics, or potent, quotable expert citations (e.g., *job creation figures related to renewable energy in the last fiscal quarter*). This ensures every argument has a solid, evidence-based backbone.
- **Identifying and Validating Credible Sources:** A core function of research AI is quality control. It analyzes indicators of source credibility, including publisher reputation, citation metrics, and linguistic tone. By cross-referencing critical claims against multiple high-authority sources, the AI can flag potential misinformation or bias, guiding the podcaster toward the most authoritative and reliable information.

- **Accelerating Understanding of Highly Complex Subjects:** AI acts as an intelligent, personalized tutor. It can take intricate theories and specialized jargon (e.g., the principles of *quantum physics*, nuances of *macroeconomic policy*) and break them down into digestible, accessible components. This ensures the host is not only informed but can confidently translate complex ideas into content that is both informative and accessible to a general audience.
- **Synthesizing Multiple Disparate Sources into Cohesive Narratives:** The AI identifies overlapping themes, contrasting viewpoints, and unique contributions from a wide variety of articles, interviews, and expert opinions. This synthesis is critical for helping the podcaster construct a balanced, nuanced narrative that reflects the full complexity of a subject.
- **Proactively Identifying Knowledge Gaps:** By analyzing the corpus of available research, the AI can highlight areas that are fundamentally underexplored, where data is scarce, or where conflicting information requires further investigation. This capability provides clear opportunities for original, groundbreaking content and unique research ideas that set the podcast apart.

3. AI for Structural Design: Building Compelling Auditory Experiences

AI plays a fundamental role in the architectural design of a podcast episode, ensuring a logical flow, smooth transitions, and a cohesive narrative—elements crucial for maximizing listener retention and satisfaction.

- **Sophisticated and Customizable Outlining Capabilities:** AI can generate comprehensive, flexible episode structures tailored to the specific content requirements, such as a 5-part structure for an analytical deep dive on *AI in healthcare ethics*. These outlines come complete with defined segment goals, suggested content, and estimated time allocations for perfect pacing.

- **Format Customization for Auditory Media:** The AI can devise suitable structural blueprints for virtually any podcast format, including linear storytelling, dynamic conversational interviews (outlining pre-interview segmentation and follow-up paths), multi-perspective panel discussions, and analytical deep dives, ensuring the structure perfectly serves the content type.
- **Fleshing out Granular Talking Points:** Within the broader segments, the AI generates specific discussion prompts, key pieces of information to be covered, counterarguments to anticipate, and potential pivots. This level of detail ensures the podcaster or interviewer is exceptionally well-prepared with granular content details and can navigate the conversation with authority and confidence.
- **Ensuring Optimal Logical and Narrative Flow:** AI guides the presentation of complex ideas in the most digestible sequence, suggesting natural transitional narratives (e.g., bridging an argument with a listener anecdote) and sequencing information for maximum intellectual and emotional impact.
- **Iterative and Dynamic Refinement:** Podcasters are not locked into the first structure. They can refine prompts and explore different structural possibilities (e.g., requesting a cyclical rather than a linear structure for a retrospective episode) for continuous flow optimization based on creative instinct or data-driven insights.

4. AI-Powered Analytics: Fostering Deeper Audience Connections and Predictive Success

AI fundamentally transforms content strategy from a reactive endeavor (analyzing what *did* work) into a proactive and predictive science (anticipating what *will* work), providing essential insights into content that deeply resonates with listeners.

- **Predictive Engagement Modeling:** AI analyzes the podcast's historical performance (downloads, retention rates, drop-off points, completion metrics) in conjunction with broader external trends (real-time search engine trends, evolving social media conversations). This capability allows the host to anticipate which topics and formats will maximize future engagement *before* a costly episode is produced.
- **Identifying High-Traction Sub-Topics and Listener Value:** The system pinpoints specific facets of a theme that consistently outperform others based on granular listener behavior. For example, it might show that listeners are highly engaged with *FIRE movement nuances* but skip segments on *budgeting basics*, guiding future content specialization.
- **Optimizing Content Format and Delivery:** AI can correlate performance data with episode structure and presentation style. It might suggest that incorporating more narrative segments, dedicated listener Q&A sections, or specific high-fidelity sound design elements could dramatically boost engagement based on quantitative data correlation.
- **Predicting Guest Response and Audience Fit:** When considering guests, AI can analyze their past media appearances, social sentiment, and content alignment with the podcast's existing top-performing themes. This helps identify individuals who are not only subject matter experts but also genuinely engaging for the specific audience demographic.
- **Identifying Underserved Segments for Expansion:** AI can highlight demographic or geographic groups where a podcast could strategically expand its reach. It then suggests content tai-

lored to the specific cultural curiosities, knowledge gaps, or language preferences of these identified groups.

- **Continuous and Adaptive Feedback Loop:** The AI models are not static; they are continuously retrained with every new piece of listener data and performance metric. This creates a virtuous, self-correcting cycle where predictions become increasingly accurate, leading to continuous refinement and optimization of the entire content strategy.

5. AI for Content Amplification: Maximizing Reach, Repurposing, and Impact

The final phase transforms a single podcast episode into a comprehensive, multi-platform content ecosystem, leveraging AI-driven repurposing to maximize reach and ROI.

- **Sophisticated Extraction of High-Value Assets:** Using advanced Natural Language Processing (NLP), AI analyzes the full episode transcript to identify key themes, recurring concepts, and high-impact, emotionally resonant soundbites. It automatically timestamps these "quotable moments" for immediate use as social media snippets, audiograms, or short video clips.
- **Theme-Based Content Expansion and Deep Dive Prompts:** The AI identifies overarching, highly valuable themes within an episode (e.g., *funding hurdles for non-profit startups* in a small business episode). These themes serve as direct prompts for creating deeper follow-up blog posts, full-length articles, or structured social media series that extend the life and value of the original content.
- **Platform-Specific Content Optimization:** The system suggests precisely how the extracted content should be formatted and packaged for maximum impact on specific target plat-

forms—recommending concise, punchy quotes and hashtags for Twitter/X, in-depth analytical insights for LinkedIn, and visually striking imagery for Instagram.

- **Streamlined Show Notes, Summaries, and SEO:** AI automatically generates comprehensive, keyword-rich summaries that are optimized for Search Engine Optimization (SEO), lists key discussion points with timestamps, and identifies relevant resources and links. This not only saves immense post-production time but significantly improves discoverability.
- **Evergreen Content Identification and Packaging:** AI pinpoints segments of an episode that contain timeless advice, foundational concepts, or perennial truths. These "evergreen" moments can be packaged as standalone content modules for consistent, long-term promotion, ensuring a steady stream of traffic and listener acquisition long after the episode's initial launch.
- **Multi-Format Creation for Diverse Learning Styles:** Beyond text and audio clips, AI assists in generating scripts for short animated explainer videos, outlines for compelling infographics, or question sets for interactive quizzes. This caters to different learning styles and platform preferences, ensuring the message reaches the widest possible audience.

By thoroughly embracing these AI-driven techniques, podcasters are empowered to ensure their shows remain dynamic, intellectually rigorous, highly engaging, and at the absolute forefront of their respective fields, effectively transforming the traditional creative and production workflow into a highly strategic, efficient, and predictive process.

5

Crafting Your Narrative with AI Scripting Tools

Artificial Intelligence (AI) has emerged not merely as a tool but as a revolutionary force for modern podcasters, fundamentally transforming the labor-intensive stages of post-production and content ideation. By automating and optimizing previously manual, time-consuming tasks, AI facilitates a shift toward efficient, sophisticated workflows. The ultimate objective is to exponentially maximize the reach and sustained impact of every episode by strategically repurposing the core content and fostering deep, continuous audience engagement across multiple platforms.

I. Strategic Content Repurposing and Expansion: The Content Multiplier

AI's foundational utility in podcasting is rooted in its sophisticated Natural Language Processing (NLP) capabilities, which allow it to analyze vast podcast transcripts with remarkable accuracy and scale, turning a single episode into a multifaceted content ecosystem.

- **Identifying Compelling Micro-Content:** AI acts as a smart editor, swiftly identifying key themes, recurring concepts, and particularly valuable, quotable soundbites. Crucially, it provides precise timestamps, automating the creation of high-impact, bite-sized content such as social media captions, visually engaging audiograms, or short-form video clips (e.g., for TikTok or Reels). This moves far beyond manual sifting, ensuring the most engaging elements are extracted and packaged efficiently.

- **Deep Theme and Takeaway Extraction:** Beyond simple quotes, AI identifies overarching thematic threads (e.g., "early-stage funding hurdles," "innovative marketing strategies," "ethical AI implications") and summarizes key takeaways. These serve as powerful prompts for developing richer, longer-form content, such as a series of in-depth blog posts, a focused email newsletter series, or even detailed follow-up podcast episodes. This ensures the intellectual property embedded in the conversation is fully leveraged and expanded upon.
- **Proactive Content Ideation and Extension:** Functioning as an intelligent "suggestion engine," AI analyzes existing content to identify related sub-topics, adjacent areas of interest, or unanswered questions that naturally stem from the original discussion. This proactive approach significantly bolsters the content calendar by ensuring a consistent flow of relevant, pre-validated material that logically extends and enriches the original discussion for returning listeners.
- **Platform-Specific Optimization and Adaptation:** Recognizing that "one size does not fit all," AI can be trained to understand the content consumption preferences, character limits, and engagement metrics of diverse social media platforms (e.g., the professional tone of LinkedIn, the rapid-fire nature of Twitter/X, the visual focus of Instagram, the video-centricity of TikTok). It suggests optimal formatting, appropriate phrasing, platform-specific calls to action, and relevant hashtags to increase the probability of content being seen, engaged with, and shared organically.

- **Evergreen Content Identification and Promotion:** AI helps isolate timeless segments—explanatory concepts, foundational advice, or historical context—within an episode. These "evergreen" snippets can be strategically packaged, cataloged, and consistently promoted as standalone resources for steady traffic and new listener acquisition long after the initial episode release, maximizing the content's lifespan and return on investment.

II. AI in Dialogue and Script Enhancement: Elevating Conversational Quality

AI moves beyond passive analysis to actively participate in the creation and refinement of spoken content, structurally and tonally elevating the quality and intellectual depth of a podcast's narrative.

- **Generating and Refining Insightful Interview Questions:** By analyzing a guest's bio, publications, past interviews, and field of expertise, AI can suggest probing, insightful, and proactive questions. It can refine existing, superficial questions to be more specific, thought-provoking, or challenging, ensuring the conversation moves beyond generic Q&A to elicit richer, more exclusive, and valuable responses for the audience.
- **Enhancing Conversational Flow and Narrative Arc:** AI is instrumental in structuring interview questions logically to create a compelling narrative arc, guiding the listener through the discussion. It can anticipate conversational threads, flag opportunities for timely follow-up questions, and suggest frameworks (such as "what if" scenarios, comparative analysis, or devil's advocate positions) that encourage deeper discussion and critical thinking, leading to a more dynamic and naturally human-sounding interview.

- **Script Polishing for Readability and Impact:** When used for scripted segments or introductions, AI acts as a sophisticated script editor. It identifies overly complex syntax, corrects subtle grammatical errors specific to spoken language, and suggests more concise, clear, and punchy alternatives. This refinement ensures the core message lands with maximum impact and minimal cognitive load for the listener, fostering intimacy and a smoother connection with the host.
- **Tone, Voice Consistency, and Lexical Variety:** AI provides critical, objective feedback on the script's intended tone (e.g., authoritative, casually humorous, empathetic, academic), suggesting vocabulary and phrasing adjustments to align perfectly with the established brand identity and host's voice. It also identifies and suggests alternatives for overused filler words or repetitive phrases, injecting welcome variety, dynamism, and polish into the dialogue.

III. Automating Post-Production and Enhancing Listener Structure

The often-tedious, manual tasks of post-production are significantly streamlined by AI, simultaneously improving production efficiency and optimizing the crucial listener experience.

- **Automated Show Notes and Comprehensive Summaries:** AI analyzes the full transcript to generate comprehensive episode summaries, systematically list key discussion points, and synthesize the episode's overall substance. This process not only saves substantial production time but also ensures the show notes are consistently accurate, highly informative, and strategically keyword-rich for improved discoverability (SEO) across podcast platforms.

- **Timestamp and Resource Extraction:** AI accurately identifies and extracts timestamps for crucial moments, allowing listeners to quickly navigate to topics of interest within the player. Furthermore, it intelligently recognizes and lists all external resources, books, websites, or contact information mentioned during the conversation, automatically transforming the show notes into a rich, navigable resource hub.
- **Crafting PIVOTAL Intros and Outros:**
    - **High-Retention Introductions:** AI generates varied and compelling **hooks** (e.g., provocative questions, startling statistics, instantly engaging soundbites) that are precisely tailored to the episode's content. This ensures the opening segment grabs audience attention immediately and clearly articulates the episode's unique value proposition, minimizing drop-off.
    - **Action-Oriented Outros:** AI assists in crafting clear, concise, and persuasive **Calls to Action (CTAs)** (e.g., subscribe on specific platforms, leave a review, visit a dedicated website, or support via patronage). It also helps summarize the episode's final key takeaways, ensuring the conversational momentum doesn't dissipate and listeners are effectively guided toward future engagement with the brand.

IV. Overcoming Creative Stagnation: AI as a Dynamic Creative Partner

AI acts as a dynamic, tireless creative partner, providing a powerful and instantaneous arsenal against writer's block, thematic fatigue, and creative stagnation.

- **Bespoke Creative Prompts and Scenarios:** AI generates intelligently crafted springboards, such as "what if" scenarios, counter-intuitive perspectives, or fictional premises based on real data, designed to ignite the podcaster's imagination and steer them toward novel, unconventional episode concepts that break formulaic trends.
- **Alternative Narrative Paths and Structures:** For podcasters following specific story arcs or content formulas, AI can propose drastically different plotlines, offer fresh thematic interpretations, or suggest alternative structural variations (e.g., shifting from a linear interview to a narrative documentary style, or restructuring a listicle into a debate format), effectively dismantling creative impasses.
- **Injecting Fresh Perspectives and Interdisciplinary Links:** AI excels at uncovering niche or interdisciplinary connections for familiar topics (e.g., linking the ethics of urban planning with principles of mental well-being, or connecting Renaissance art history with modern supply chain logistics). This ensures content remains perpetually engaging, deeply insightful, and moves consistently beyond superficial or widely-covered treatments.
- **Dynamic Dialogue and Creator Collaboration:** The creative process becomes an iterative loop: the podcaster provides the initial context and unique vision, the AI quickly offers a wealth of tailored possibilities and structural suggestions, and the creator refines and finalizes them. This symbiotic relationship ensures a consistent and high-velocity output of polished, high-quality content without sacrificing the unique human voice, critical insight, and singular vision of the creator.

In essence, AI serves as an intelligent content multiplier and workflow accelerator, transforming the rich, nuanced, and ephemeral conversations of a podcast into a permanent, comprehensive, and multi-format content ecosystem. By strategically embracing and integrating this technology, podcasters can unlock the full, often untapped potential of their episodes, making the entire creation, production, and distribution process demonstrably more manageable, significantly more effective, and ultimately, profoundly more successful.

6

The Art of Recording: Capturing Your Best Audio

The pursuit of professional-grade podcast audio, especially when capturing dynamic events with multiple contributors—whether in a bustling studio or across global digital links—is fundamentally rooted in the discipline of multi-track recording. This sophisticated technique involves dedicating a unique, isolated recording channel to every distinct sound source. The payoff for this methodical approach is unprecedented control, flexibility, and quality in the critical post-production phase, transforming raw, chaotic audio into a polished, impactful listening experience that captivates and retains the audience.

The Multi-Track Advantage: The Foundation of Professional Audio

Multi-track recording is not merely a convenience; it is the essential bedrock upon which all high-fidelity audio production is built, offering an unparalleled surgical precision in editing and mixing. Its core benefits directly address the challenges of managing multiple, often unpredictable, human voices and acoustic environments:

- **Granular Individual Level Control (The Mixing Power):** Unlike a single-track mixed recording, which locks all sound sources into an inseparable, uneditable waveform, multi-tracking allows the editor to make microscopic volume adjustments for each speaker or performer. This guarantees that quiet, reflective moments from one participant can be brought forward *independently* without causing a boisterous speaker's track to clip or become overwhelmingly dominant. The editor can establish a consistent, even acoustic presence for every voice, ensuring a cohesive and perfectly balanced auditory experience throughout the entire episode, regardless of the speakers' natural volume variations.

- **Targeted Noise Reduction and Equalization (EQ) (The Surgical Fix):** A persistent, distracting noise—such as a fan's hum, a distant siren, a computer's whir, or even chair squeaks—may only be present on one speaker's microphone due to their unique acoustic environment. With multi-track separation, a precise noise reduction filter or targeted EQ can be applied *only* to that specific track, eliminating the distraction without thinning the sound, introducing artifacts, or dulling the clarity and warmth of the other participants' voices. This isolation is crucial for maintaining the sonic integrity of the entire podcast.
- **Precision Management of Vocal Artifacts (Sibilance and Plosives):** Unwanted vocal sounds are a common hazard, and multi-track recording provides the tools for surgical correction:

    - **Sibilance** (the harsh, whistling "s" and "sh" sounds, often caused by microphone proximity or overly bright EQ) can be tamed using a specialized **de-esser** effect. Crucially, this effect is often placed only on the track of the speaker who exhibits the issue, preventing the de-esser from dulling or lisping the sibilants of the other speakers who may not need the processing.
    - **Plosives** (the explosive "p," "b," and occasionally "t" sounds caused by a puff of air hitting the microphone di-

aphragm) can be surgically reduced using high-pass filters (to cut the low-frequency energy of the blast) or corrective EQ without compromising the warmth and body of the other voices. Physical prevention with a **pop filter** remains the first line of defense.

- **Seamless and Surgical Editing (The Workflow Accelerator):** Multi-track files dramatically simplify and speed up the editing workflow. An unwanted, non-verbal interruption—such as a cough, a disruptive sneeze, a heavy sigh, or the clatter of a coffee cup—can be instantly muted on the *single track* where it occurred, leaving the flow and continuity of the conversation from the other tracks completely undisturbed. Furthermore, multi-track separation enables sophisticated pacing adjustments, such as smoothly tightening pauses, rearranging conversational segments, or overlapping clips for dynamic, radio-style effect, all while ensuring the natural flow is preserved.
- **Creative Stereo Mixing and Sound Design (The Immersive Experience):** For a more immersive listening experience, multi-track provides the freedom for creative mixing. Voices or instruments can be strategically **panned** (positioned) in the stereo field (left-to-right), giving listeners a sense of physical space or separation between speakers, making it easier to follow who is talking. Furthermore, unique sonic effects, such as dramatic reverb, subtle delay, or production music/sound effects, can be applied to specific tracks or layered beneath the dialogue for dramatic impact without muddying the entire mix or interfering with vocal clarity.

In-Person Live Recording: Orchestrating the Studio Sound

Capturing a live, multi-contributor event in a physical space presents unique acoustic and hardware challenges that must be systematically managed. Success hinges on a meticulous approach to signal flow, gain structure, and sound isolation:

1. **Essential Hardware & Signal Flow:** The core of the in-person setup is the **Digital Audio Workstation (DAW)** (e.g., Pro Tools, Logic Pro, Adobe Audition, Reaper) running on a powerful computer, and a high-quality **multi-channel audio interface** or digital mixer. *Crucially*, this device must have enough discrete inputs to physically accommodate every single microphone, with each microphone routed to its own dedicated, unique track within the DAW. The quality of the built-in **microphone preamplifiers** (preamps), which boost the microphone's tiny signal to a usable level, is paramount for clean audio gain and a low noise floor.
2. **Mastering Gain Staging:** Setting the input amplification (**gain**) is the single most critical step before recording. Ask each participant to speak at their normal, expected volume (and also a bit louder, to simulate an enthusiastic moment). The gain must be adjusted so that the input meter peaks consistently within the ideal **sweet spot of -12dB to -6dB** on the digital meter. This careful setting ensures maximum signal-to-noise ratio (a louder signal than the self-noise of the equipment) while providing ample **headroom**—the crucial buffer zone needed to prevent unexpected loud sounds (like a laugh or an exclamation) from *clipping* (distorting irrevocably due to exceeding the digital limit of 0dBFS).
3. **Strategic Use of Directional Microphones:** To mitigate **sound bleed** (or *cross-talk*—where one speaker's voice is picked up by another's microphone) and minimize ambient room noise, directional microphones are mandatory. **Cardioid-pattern microphones** are the standard choice, as they are highly sensitive to sound directly in front of the capsule and actively reject sound arriving from the sides and rear. This acoustic isolation is vital for

achieving the clean separation necessary for effective multi-track editing. For greater isolation in challenging environments, **super-cardioid** or **hypercardioid** patterns may be employed, though they require stricter mic placement discipline.

4. **Critical and Continuous Monitoring:** The non-negotiable use of **high-quality, closed-back headphones** by the audio engineer (and preferably the host) is essential. Closed-back designs prevent the monitoring sound from leaking back into the live microphones, which can cause phase cancellation or feedback loops. The engineer must actively and *critically* monitor each individual channel—not just the final combined mix—to immediately identify and correct issues such as clipping, unwanted persistent background noise, intermittent signal loss, or microphone rub before they ruin the take.
5. **Anticipating Dynamic Range:** Given the unpredictable nature of human conversation, always set gain conservatively. It is infinitely better to record a track slightly too quiet (which can be cleanly amplified in post-production using a process called normalization or gain adjustment) than to record it too loud and distorted (clipped), which is a digital ruin impossible to fix. The engineer must allow for the natural dynamic range of speakers, from a quiet, intimate reflection to a sudden, passionate exclamation, without ever risking digital distortion.

Remote Multi-Participant Sessions: Bridging the Digital Divide with Quality

Remote collaboration introduces the acute challenges of internet latency, unstable connections, varying home acoustic environments, and consumer-grade equipment. Dedicated platforms have evolved to use a sophisticated, two-pronged strategy that bypasses the limitations of live streaming:

- **The Power of Local Recording Technology (The Double-Ender):** Modern, dedicated remote recording platforms (such as Zencastr, Riverside.fm, or SquadCast) utilize the principle of **double-ender recording**. They instruct the participant's own computer to record their audio directly and locally, capturing the sound *at the source*. This process captures pristine, high-resolution audio files (often 48kHz WAV or high-quality MP3) that are entirely insulated from the inevitable quality degradation, momentary drops, packet loss, or latency issues inherent in the live internet stream used for monitoring.
- **Separate and Synchronized File Upload:** Immediately following the recording session, these platforms automatically manage the secure upload of the individual, high-quality audio files from each participant's local computer to a central server. The result is a set of synchronized, discrete audio files for every single speaker, perfectly ready for multi-track mixing within the DAW, just as if they had recorded in the same professional studio room.
- **Essential Guest Preparation and Acoustic Control:** The quality of the final product is often determined by the weakest link—the guest's environment and setup. Proactively instructing guests on best practices is paramount:

    - **Microphone:** Strongly encourage the use of a decent external USB microphone (like a Blue Yeti or Rode NT-USB), or at least a high-quality headset microphone, and emphatically avoid built-in laptop or webcam microphones, which introduce excessive room noise and poor fidelity.
    - **Acoustics:** Instruct the guest to record in the quietest space available, ideally one with soft furnishings (carpets, curtains, bookshelves, or even a closet full of clothes) to minimize echo, harsh reflections, and room reverb.

    - **Bandwidth:** Advise guests to close all unnecessary applications (email, social media, streaming services, background downloads) that consume internet bandwidth to ensure a stable, low-latency connection for the monitoring/communication stream.
- **The Pre-Session Soundcheck Protocol:** A crucial investment of time, a 10-15 minute dedicated pre-session soundcheck is mandatory, not optional. This is the time to test and confirm audio levels for every participant, listen critically for any persistent background noises in their environment, and confirm a stable video/audio connection for real-time interaction. It also serves as an opportunity to coach the guest on microphone technique (e.g., staying close to the mic).
- **Managing Conversation Flow in the Absence of Visual Cues:** Internet delay (**latency**) and lack of immediate visual feedback can lead to participants inadvertently talking over one another. The host must actively guide the conversation by:

    - Using **verbal transition phrases** to clearly signal when a speaker's turn is complete ("That's a great point, what do you think, John?").
    - Allowing for **brief, strategic pauses** (2-3 seconds) after a speaker finishes to compensate for potential lag and signal an open floor.
    - Employing **sparing verbal affirmations** ("yes," "mhm," "I see") to acknowledge the speaker without injecting distracting background noise onto the main conversation track. If possible, a dedicated back-channel for non-verbal cues (like a chat box) should be used instead of interjections.

Advanced Techniques for Polished Audio and Seamless Workflow

For the discerning podcaster and audio engineer seeking to achieve true broadcast quality, these advanced practices provide an additional layer of control and refinement that separates amateur productions from professional ones:

- **The Utility of Room Tone (The Silence Filler):** Before the conversation begins or immediately after it concludes, record a minute or two of the absolute quiet of the recording space—this is the **room tone** or **ambience track**. This recording captures the subtle, unique, low-level acoustic fingerprint (the hum of the AC, the distant city sound, the preamps' self-noise). In post-production, short snippets of room tone can be strategically inserted to naturally fill awkward silences, smooth out the abrupt start and stop of edits, and prevent the disconcerting, unnatural effect of "dead silence" that can sometimes follow a hard edit, which makes the audience aware of the edit.
- **Latency Compensation and Track Alignment:** In complex remote collaborations, especially involving music or very tight conversational edits, minor internet-induced delays (**latency**) can cause tracks to be slightly misaligned by milliseconds. Professional DAWs feature **track delay compensation** tools that use timestamps embedded in the locally recorded files to automatically shift and align the multi-track files to ensure perfect, phase-accurate synchronization, making it sound as if everyone was in the same room.
- **Click Tracks for Tempo Consistency:** Essential for any musical performance, intro/outro segments, or any voice-over that requires rhythmic precision, a **click track** (metronome) is generated by the DAW and distributed via headphones to all performers. This guarantees a consistent tempo that is locked to

the session's clock, which simplifies the process of overdubbing, adding music, or mixing with timed sound effects later.

- **Shock Mounts and Isolation:** Even subtle, physical vibrations from a desk (a foot tap, a hand resting heavily on the surface, or the rumble of external traffic) can transmit as a disruptive, low-frequency **rumble** or *thump* through the microphone stand. **Shock mounts**—elastic cradle systems—isolate sensitive condenser and dynamic microphones from these structural vibrations, preserving the clarity and warmth of the voice while eliminating distracting subsonic noise.
- **The Non-Negotiable Backup Plan (Redundancy):** Technology, even the most reliable, can fail. A professional recording setup always incorporates a **redundancy plan** to ensure the session is never lost. This might involve running a secondary, local stereo recording on the host's computer simultaneously with the primary multi-track system, or using a dedicated, standalone hardware recorder (like a Zoom or Tascam unit) to capture an independent, failsafe track. This "belt-and-suspenders" approach mitigates the risk of software crashes, power outages, or data corruption.

By diligently mastering these multi-track recording principles and proactively managing the inherent challenges of both physical and digital recording environments, podcasters can guarantee that their dynamic content is captured with maximal clarity, professional impact, and a quality that truly honors the message they are seeking to convey.

7

The Evolving Landscape of Podcast Production

The creation of a truly professional-grade podcast episode now sits at a dynamic and complex intersection where the time-honored principles of traditional audio engineering meet the transformative power of cutting-edge artificial intelligence. While the foundational and ultimate granular control over the sonic narrative still firmly resides within the **Digital Audio Workstation (DAW)**, the efficiency, speed, and attainable quality of post-production are being fundamentally and dramatically redefined by sophisticated, AI-powered tools. Understanding and mastering this dual-environment workflow is no longer optional but essential for the modern podcaster. The DAW remains the definitive digital studio—the non-negotiable workspace where every advanced, AI-assisted edit, restoration, and polish must ultimately be reviewed, meticulously finalized, and precision-mixed to broadcast standard.

Part 1: The Essential Role of the Digital Audio Workstation (DAW) in Podcast Editing

The DAW is far more than a simple recording program; it serves as the comprehensive, multi-layered digital control panel that provides the absolute, granular precision needed to sculpt raw, unrefined audio into a polished, compelling, and effortless listening experience. While AI undeniably offers powerful automation capabilities that save countless hours, the **foundational skills of manual, meticulous editing within a DAW remain crucial** for maintaining creative, nuanced control and for expertly troubleshooting unique or complex audio issues that automated systems might misinterpret.

Core DAW Functions for a Clean, Coherent Timeline

Effective podcast editing is fundamentally a rigorous, meticulous process of intelligent subtraction, precise arrangement, and subtle sonic enhancement, all aimed at achieving a seamless, invisible flow for the listener. This entire process is driven by the mastery of a few core DAW functions and concepts:

- **Understanding the Waveform: The Editor's Visual Map** The waveform—the graphical, visual representation of your audio's amplitude (its perceived loudness) plotted over time—is the editor's single most important guide and diagnostic tool. Distinct, predictable patterns in the waveform immediately flag different types of sounds and sonic events: smooth, consistent, and gently rolling shapes indicate clear, stable speech; near-flat lines represent true silence or low-level room tone; and sharp, erratic, high-amplitude spikes typically signify unwanted transient noises like distracting clicks, mouth pops, loud breaths, or sudden external sounds. Precision editing, which is key to unnoticeable cuts, is achieved by visually aligning the cut points *precisely* to these specific visual cues.
- **Cutting/Splitting and Deleting: The Surgical Approach** This foundational function empowers the editor to divide an audio clip at hyper-specific points to isolate and remove unwanted

segments. This might involve excising a full sentence mistake, a lengthy filler word ("um," "uh," "like"), or a noisy external interruption. Once the unwanted segment is isolated and deleted, the DAW's ability to automatically and cleanly **"ripple edit"** (a feature that slides the subsequent audio forward to perfectly close the resulting gap) is crucial for maintaining flow. Furthermore, the DAW often applies a subtle, microscopic **crossfade** at the newly created seam, which gradually blends the audio on either side of the cut to prevent an audible, jarring transition or a percussive "pop."

- **Trimming: Refining the Edges**
  Trimming involves shortening an audio clip by dragging its start or end point inward. This technique is invaluable for removing the inevitable "dead air" before a speaker begins a thought, eliminating trailing sounds at the end of a sentence (such as a subtle sigh, an audible chair squeak, or a swallow), and generally tightening the overall pacing of the dialogue by ensuring spoken phrases begin and end promptly and cleanly.
- **Moving and Rearranging: Structuring the Narrative**
  The intuitive ability to drag and drop audio clips freely onto any track on the timeline is vital for complex structural and narrative editing. This is used extensively in **comping** (the art of compiling the best, mistake-free portions of multiple takes into a single cohesive, flawless performance track) or for simply moving a sentence, a paragraph, or an entire section to a more logical, impactful position in the narrative flow that was not captured during the original recording.

Refining the Audio: Pacing, Noise, and Room Tone Management

Beyond the basic, necessary function of cutting and arrangement, the DAW provides the sophisticated tools required to enhance listening comfort, maximize clarity, and deliver professional polish:

- **Removing Long Pauses and Controlling Pacing:** Pacing is arguably the most paramount element for listener engagement. Excessive silence, which is clearly visible as flat, low-amplitude sections on the waveform, can make a podcast feel slow, draggy, or amateurish. These pauses must be aggressively and strategically managed, either by trimming them down to a more natural, brief, conversational pause (e.g., a deliberate 500ms to 1-second breath pause) or cutting them out entirely and moving the subsequent audio forward to relentlessly maintain conversational momentum.
- **Excising Extraneous Sounds and Applying Room Tone:** Non-verbal utterances (coughs, sniffles, throat clearing, mouth noises) and brief background noises are easily identified as sharp, distinct spikes in the waveform. These are surgically isolated and deleted. A critical, professional technique for achieving smooth, unnoticeable edits is the strategic application of **room tone**—the subtle, continuous, non-speech ambient sound of the recording environment itself. By subtly layering a short, repeated clip of room tone beneath an edited section, the editor prevents the resulting "hole" from sounding "dead" or unnaturally abrupt, ensuring that the edit is aurally invisible and the listener's focus remains on the content.
- **Multi-Track Editing for Complex Recordings:** The majority of modern, conversational podcasts involve multiple speakers, requiring the core use of the DAW's multi-track capability. This setup is indispensable because it allows each speaker's audio to be treated as an independent stream or track. For example, if Speaker A coughs loudly, their individual track can be instantly muted for the duration of the cough without af-

fecting the dialogue on the other speakers' tracks. It also enables the precise temporal alignment of different audio streams, which is critical for compensating for any network latency or minor hardware sync issues that may have occurred during the remote or in-studio recording.

- **Volume Consistency: Gain, Fades, and De-essing:** The DAW provides the fundamental tools for all dynamic and volume control. Adjusting **gain** ensures consistent, matched volume levels between different speakers, interview segments, or advertising breaks. **Fade-in** and **fade-out** functions are essential for gracefully and professionally introducing and concluding music, sound effects, or segment bumpers. Finally, **De-essing**, typically applied using a dedicated specialized plugin within the DAW's effects rack, is used to dynamically and intelligently reduce harsh, abrasive, high-frequency 's' and 't' sounds (known as sibilance) that can be painful, distracting, or fatiguing to the listener.

Part 2: AI for Audio Restoration and Noise Reduction

Artificial Intelligence has fundamentally transformed the traditionally labor-intensive and highly technical process of audio repair and restoration. AI tools leverage sophisticated machine learning models, trained on massive, diverse datasets of clean speech and various noise profiles, to intelligently and accurately differentiate the desired signal (the voice) from the unwanted noise with surgical precision.

Targeting Noise Types with Surgical Precision

AI's inherent ability to analyze the complex spectral fingerprint of sound—the sound's component frequencies—allows for highly effective, targeted reduction that surpasses traditional filtering methods:

- **Broadband Noise/Hiss Removal:** This common issue, often originating from less expensive microphone preamplifiers or older analog gear, is characterized by a wide, pervasive spectral fingerprint. Traditional static filters often introduce unpleasant "underwater" or "phasiness" artifacts. AI, however, intelligently identifies the spectral signature of the hiss itself and *subtracts* it with remarkable clarity and minimal collateral damage, preserving the natural timbre and tone of the voice.
- **Hum Detection and Removal:** Electrical hums (50 Hz or 60 Hz fundamental tones and their associated harmonic overtones) are a persistent studio and field recording problem. AI can automatically and rapidly detect the specific, precise frequencies associated with the hum and generate a corresponding, highly precise notch filter to eliminate them, often working dynamically in real-time or near-real-time.
- **Transient Noises Isolation:** Short-lived, sharp, percussive noises—like a door closing, a chair squeak, a phone vibration, or a distant siren—are notoriously difficult to remove manually without inevitably affecting the surrounding speech. Advanced AI spectral editing techniques can visually map and algorithmically isolate these distinct transient sounds, enabling their surgical removal with minimal perceptible impact on the critical dialogue track.
- **Room Echo/Reverb Reduction (De-reverb):** In acoustically untreated or reflective acoustic environments (e.g., a large office or kitchen), wall and surface reflections cause dialogue to sound "muddy," hollow, or distant. Specialized AI de-reverb tools analyze the room's unique acoustic fingerprint and significantly attenuate the unwanted reflections, effectively "drying up" the

sound and bringing the speaker's voice forward to sound much more present and immediate, as if recorded in a professional booth.

Streamlined and Accessible Workflow

The primary, undeniable benefit of these AI audio restoration tools is the radical simplification of a historically complex process. By analyzing a brief **noise profile** (a small snippet of audio containing *only* the specific noise without any speech), the AI quickly learns its characteristic properties and applies a targeted, dynamic reduction algorithm across the entire recording. This dramatically reduces the time spent on clean-up and makes professional-grade audio restoration and clarity accessible to all podcasters, including those who lack deep technical expertise in traditional spectral editing and complex outboard gear.

Part 3: Intelligent AI-Assisted Editing for Vocal Clarity

The most recent and significant innovation lies in AI's capacity to refine the nuance of human speech itself, specifically by automating the tedious, repetitive task of removing common vocal imperfections while critically ensuring that the final output remains natural, authentic, and maintains the speaker's intended rhythm.

Automated Imperfection Removal

AI leverages powerful technologies, including **Natural Language Processing (NLP)** and advanced acoustic analysis, to meticulously detect, classify, and target specific human speech artifacts:

- **Filler Words:** Sophisticated NLP models are exceptionally effective at accurately identifying and deleting common verbal tics and hesitation markers such as "um," "uh," "like," "so," and "you know." These can be removed with great speed to tighten the dialogue flow, increase listener attention, and eliminate distractions.
- **Long Pauses:** Algorithms can intelligently flag and automatically trim any silences that exceed a pre-defined duration (e.g., flagging any pause longer than 1.5 seconds) to a more acceptable, conversational length (e.g., 500ms to 750ms).
- **Stumbles and False Starts:** AI pinpoints the exact moments where a speaker corrects themselves mid-sentence or makes a clear verbal mistake, offering quick, suggested removal edits that can be executed with a single click.
- **Mouth Noises:** Highly sophisticated AI analysis can accurately distinguish the sharp, percussive sounds of lip smacks, tongue clicks, and other non-speech mouth noises from actual spoken phonemes. This allows the AI to isolate and remove them for a remarkably cleaner, non-fatiguing listening experience.

Configurability and the Human-in-the-Loop Workflow

The true power and practical utility of these AI editing tools are contingent on their ability to be fine-tuned and controlled by the editor. Users must be able to adjust the *sensitivity* of detection for each specific artifact type. A low sensitivity might miss genuine, distracting "ums," while an overly high sensitivity could accidentally remove natural hesitation or a deliberate, dramatic pause, resulting in dialogue that sounds unnatural, unnervingly fast, or "robotic."

The universally recommended and best-practice approach is the **human-in-the-loop** workflow. The AI is utilized to provide suggestions, flag potential edits, and perform the initial, time-consuming heavy lifting, but the human editor maintains crucial, final oversight. They review the AI's suggested edits to ensure that the speaker's natural rhythm, character, and intended meaning are scrupulously preserved, overriding any automated edits that compromise the authenticity or clarity of the conversation.

Part 4: AI for Leveling and Mastering: Achieving Professional Sonic Consistency

Mastering is the critical final stage of audio production—a crucial, technical step that ensures the podcast is optimally prepared for broadcast and distribution. AI mastering tools now automatically enforce industry-wide loudness standards and apply subtle tonal shaping for universal playback consistency across diverse platforms.

- **LUFS Compliance for Volume Standardization:** AI mastering tools automatically analyze and normalize the audio to precisely meet specific **Loudness Units Full Scale (LUFS)** targets (e.g., the current industry standard of -16 LUFS for stereo podcasts and -19 LUFS for mono/single-channel audio). LUFS is the standardized international measure of *perceived* loudness, designed to represent how the human ear hears volume. This compliance eliminates drastic, unprofessional volume shifts between different segments or episodes and, crucially, prevents the audio from being so loud that it gets aggressively volume-compressed or limited by streaming services (like Spotify or Apple Podcasts), a process which can severely degrade overall sonic quality.
- **Tonal Balance and Cohesion (EQ and Compression):** AI applies intelligent, dynamic **equalization (EQ)** to automatically correct common spectral issues, such as a prominent, distracting low-end "mud" or weak, undefined high-end "air,"

ensuring that voices are consistently clear, rich, and tonally balanced. It also utilizes sophisticated **compression** to optimally reduce the overall dynamic range (the often-large difference between the loudest and quietest parts). This compression is absolutely vital as it makes loud parts slightly quieter and quiet parts slightly louder, providing a crucial sense of **cohesion ("glue")** to the overall mix that is the hallmark of professional, broadcast-quality audio.

- **Accessibility and Efficiency of Broadcast Quality:** AI mastering democratizes professional-grade audio by offering a rapid, simple, and extremely cost-effective way to achieve broadcast quality without requiring a dedicated mastering engineer. By freeing creators from complex, technical manipulation of esoteric audio parameters, it ensures a consistent and professional sound across all episodes—a factor vital for building listener trust, reducing listener fatigue, and reinforcing a strong brand identity.

Part 5: AI Transcription for Editing, SEO, and Accessibility

AI-driven transcription services are an indispensable, non-audio tool that fundamentally enhances workflow, discoverability, and audience reach by converting the spoken word into highly accurate text with remarkable speed.

- **Accelerated Editing Workflow (Searchable Audio):** High-quality transcripts instantly transform the linear, time-based audio timeline into a flexible, searchable text document. This allows editors to use simple text search functions (Ctrl+F) to instantly locate a keyword, a specific phrase, or the discussion of a particular topic. This dramatically speeds up the process of making precise cuts, rearranging large segments, or identifying long sections for complete removal, saving substantial time compared to the tedious process of scrubbing through audio to find a specific moment.

- **Enhanced Discoverability (SEO):**
The act of publishing a full, keyword-rich transcript or generating detailed, descriptive show notes derived directly from the transcript allows powerful search engines (like Google and Bing) to index the podcast content as written text. This crucial step turns passive, ephemeral audio into actively searchable, discoverable web content, enabling new audience discovery by users performing routine web searches. This capability is a primary driver of organic new audience growth and long-tail traffic.
- **Accessibility and Content Repurposing:**
Transcripts provide crucial accessibility for the deaf or hard of hearing, a vital necessity often mandated by inclusive content practices and ethical guidelines. They also cater to diverse listening preferences (e.g., allowing a user to read a transcript in a noisy environment where listening is difficult). Furthermore, the transcribed text is the foundational raw material for effortless **content repurposing**—this includes creating multiple blog posts, generating quotable text for social media graphics, or producing perfectly synchronized video subtitles—maximizing the return on investment and the overall reach of every single minute of recorded audio. The time savings from AI transcription alone can amount to well over a hundred hours per year for weekly podcasters.

8

Music, Sound Effects, and AI Sound Design

The integration of Artificial Intelligence in generating music, sound effects, and ambient soundscapes marks a revolutionary shift in audio production for podcasts. While this technology offers unprecedented creative flexibility and efficiency, it simultaneously introduces a complex web of legal, ethical, and commercial considerations. Podcasters and audio producers must adopt a rigorous due diligence process to ensure their commercial projects are legally compliant and ethically sound.1. The Critical Imperative of Licensing and Commercial Use

The foundational pillar of legally using AI-generated audio is securing the appropriate **licensing**. AI audio platforms are primarily driven by commercial models that employ tiered licensing structures, dictating the scope of usage rights based on the user's subscription level or specific asset purchase.

- **Meticulous Scrutiny of Licensing Agreements:** It is non-negotiable to thoroughly review and comprehend the provider's Terms of Service (TOS) and End-User License Agreements (EULA). Creators must unequivocally understand the platform's definition of "commercial use," which typically encompasses any project intended for monetization, including ad-supported podcasts, promotional clips, or branded content. A free or trial tier almost universally restricts usage to non-commercial, personal projects, necessitating a paid subscription for any professional or revenue-generating application.

- **Deconstructing the "Royalty-Free" Misconception:** The term "royalty-free" is frequently misunderstood. It signifies that the user is not required to make recurring payment installments (royalties) to the AI model creator or the original data source for each playback or distribution. However, this designation **does not** imply the license is unrestricted. The creator must verify critical limitations:
    - **Scope of Use:** Are there caps on distribution volume or audience size?
    - **Modification Rights:** Are you permitted to edit, loop, remix, or otherwise alter the generated audio?
    - **Geographical and Duration Limits:** Is the license perpetual (for the lifetime of the project) and worldwide, or is it time-bound or regionally restricted?
    - **Exclusive vs. Non-Exclusive:** Virtually all AI audio licenses are non-exclusive, meaning the platform can license the same audio to countless other users.
- **The Gravity of Non-Compliance:** Ignoring or misunderstanding licensing stipulations constitutes a direct breach of contract and a violation of copyright law. The consequences are severe, including formal DMCA takedown notices, content removal from hosting platforms (Spotify, Apple Podcasts), account termination, and potential civil legal action for copyright infringement, demanding compensatory damages and legal fees.
- **Evaluating Platform Ownership Policies:** Podcasters should favor platforms that offer the most expansive and unambiguous transfer of commercial rights to the user. Some providers may retain full ownership of the underlying generation model and only grant a limited use license, while others grant the user

broad ownership rights to the final, generated output. This distinction is paramount for long-term project security.

2. The Dynamic Challenge of AI Copyright and Authorship

Copyright law, established to protect the original works of **human authors**, currently faces a profound challenge from purely AI-generated content. This area of law is rapidly evolving, requiring creators to stay informed.

- **The Human Authorship Doctrine:** In major legal jurisdictions, most notably the United States, the prerequisite for copyright protection remains human creativity. Audio generated *entirely* by an AI algorithm, without substantial, discernable human creative direction or editing, is often deemed uncopyrightable. Such works may technically fall into the public domain, making them free for anyone to use, which undermines the creator's ability to defend their work against copying.
- **Establishing the Creator's Role as "Author":** The key to establishing a claim of copyright or usage rights rests on the human user's creative involvement. Stronger claims are built on:

    - **Detailed and Curated Prompting:** The specificity, originality, and creative intent embedded in the text prompts and parameter settings.
    - **Iterative Refinement:** The process of generating multiple options and exercising creative judgment to select the best output.
    - **Substantive Editing and Post-Production:** Applying human-driven arrangement, mastering, or layering with other elements (e.g., mixing the AI-generated music with voiceovers or non-AI sound effects). This transforms

the raw output into a derivative work with human authorship.

- **The Criticality of Record Keeping:** To successfully defend a claim of usage rights or authorship, creators must maintain meticulous documentation of their process. This includes saving all original prompts, recording the date and time of generation, documenting the specific parameters used, and logging all subsequent human edits and modifications. This evidence establishes the user's creative contribution.
- **Mitigating the Risk of Algorithmic Infringement:** AI models are trained on massive datasets, some of which may contain copyrighted music. There is an inherent, albeit small, risk that the AI may inadvertently generate an output that is *substantially similar* to an existing copyrighted work—a concept known as algorithmic or derivative infringement. For high-stakes commercial projects, a basic due diligence check—listening for striking similarity to well-known music—is a prudent risk management step before final release.

3. Ethical and Best Practices for Attribution and Transparency

Even when a license legally defines the audio as "royalty-free" and does not explicitly mandate attribution, responsible practices and transparency are vital components of ethical content creation and community good faith.

- **Adhering to Stated Attribution Requirements:** The first step is absolute compliance with the AI platform's specific requirements, which may be a simple credit in the show notes, a visual mention in video accompaniments, or even a brief audible credit within the podcast itself.
- **The Power of Transparent Acknowledgement:** Where no strict guideline exists, adopting a policy of transparent acknowl-

edgment is highly recommended. A general credit, such as "Intro music generated by [AI Platform Name] and edited by [Creator Name]" or "Select sound effects created using [AI Tool]," serves several beneficial purposes:

- It informs the audience, contributing to an open dialogue about the intersection of AI and artistic production.
- It demonstrates the creator's commitment to ethical transparency.
- It provides a clear source of origin, simplifying the process of resolving any potential future licensing or copyright inquiries.

Summary of Essential Creator Diligence for AI Audio Integration

To confidently and legally integrate AI-generated audio into a commercial podcast, creators must integrate the following proactive and informed principles into their production workflow:

1. **Thorough License Review:** Secure a complete understanding of the license terms, specifically confirming rights for commercial use, modification privileges, and the duration and territory of the rights granted.
2. **Document Creative Input:** Systematically record all prompts, chosen parameters, and human editing steps to solidify the claim of human authorship and usage rights.
3. **Meticulous Compliance:** Strictly follow all specified attribution, usage, and distribution requirements set forth by the AI audio provider.
4. **Validate Commercial Use:** Prior to the official distribution of any episode or advertisement, confirm that the chosen license tier explicitly covers the specific media (podcast, video, social me-

dia ad), the intended territory (worldwide vs. local), and the expected duration of the project.

5. **Seek Clarification:** If any term in the EULA or TOS appears ambiguous, immediately contact the AI audio provider's support team for written clarification and permanently archive all correspondence.

By adopting this disciplined and proactive approach, creators can harness the immense creative potential of AI-generated audio while ensuring their work remains fully compliant with the law and aligns with the highest ethical standards of the podcasting community.

9

Generating Complete Podcast Audio with AI

The world of audio production is undergoing a profound transformation, driven by the exponential advancements in AI voice synthesis, commonly known as Text-to-Speech (TTS) technology. The era of the monotonous, robotic voice is over. Today's neural AI generators produce speech that is astonishingly natural, nuanced, and rich with human qualities, complete with authentic emotional depth, sophisticated pacing, and distinct regional accents. This technological leap democratizes high-quality audio creation, offering podcasters an unprecedented array of tools for flexibility, massive scalability, and creative control over their sonic identity.I. The Core Mechanics and Expansive Applications of Advanced AI Voices

How AI Voice Synthesis Works: A Deep Dive into Neural Networks

The foundation of modern AI voices lies in advanced machine learning, specifically deep learning and neural networks. These models are trained on colossal, meticulously curated datasets of professional human speech—often thousands of hours of high-fidelity recordings. The AI does more than just stitch together recorded words; it deconstructs and learns the intricate *rules* of human communication: the subtleties of phoneme pronunciation, the interplay of pitch (intonation), the rhythm (prosody), and the specific vocalic texture (timbre) that defines a voice. Modern systems, particularly those using transformer architectures, reconstruct this speech synthetically. The result is generative audio that is nearly indistinguishable from a human voice actor, capable of dynamically adjusting its delivery based on the script's semantic context.

Diverse and Transformative Applications in Podcasting:

- **Scalable and Consistent Narration:** AI provides an elegant solution for solo creators, niche content producers, or anyone requiring massive, consistent content output. An AI narrator can provide high-quality, fatigue-free narration for an entire library or ongoing series. This consistency is a major branding advantage. It makes production for historically cost-prohibitive formats—such as daily news digests, educational course material, or extensive lore deep-dives—financially and logistically viable.
- **Dynamic Character Vocalization for Audio Dramas:** In the realm of audio fiction, AI is revolutionary. It allows writers to populate their stories with a rich, expansive cast of characters without the constraints of booking multiple human actors. Creators can select a base voice and meticulously customize parameters to craft unique personas. This includes defining specific vocal traits (e.g., a formal, authoritative narrator; a high-pitched, fast-talking sidekick; a slow, gravelly voice for a non-human entity). AI ensures that these characters sound consistent across every scene and episode.
- **Streamlined and Rapid Production Cycles:** AI dramatically accelerates the production timeline. It eliminates the logistical complexity of casting, managing recording sessions, and homogenizing uneven audio quality from remote human recordings. A single producer can instantly assign various AI voices to dialogue in a script, generating an entire, perfectly clean scene in

minutes. This rapid iteration allows for extensive A/B testing of scripts and quicker turnaround times for time-sensitive content.

- **Content Repurposing and Multi-Platform Expansion:** AI voices are the engine for transforming existing written content—including detailed blog posts, technical research papers, e-books, or long-form social media threads—into engaging audio articles or full podcast episodes. This maximizes the return on existing content investment by broadening reach to new listener demographics who prefer passive consumption, commuting, or multitasking.
- **Advanced Emotional Expressiveness and Delivery:** The most sophisticated AI voices are trained to convey a broad spectrum of human emotions (e.g., excitement, despair, skepticism, urgency, calm authority). They modulate fundamental characteristics like tone, pitch contour, and speaking cadence based on context clues within the script or through explicit markup language (tags like [SADLY] or [URGENT]) inserted by the creator, ensuring a believable and deeply engaging storytelling experience.

II. Strategic Selection and Granular Customization

The selection of an AI voice is not merely a technical step; it is a fundamental brand decision. The voice is the show's primary personality, profoundly influencing audience perception, trust, and connection. It must be technically impeccable and perfectly align with the podcast's narrative theme and target audience.

Crucial Selection Criteria for an AI Voice:

- **Audio Fidelity and Naturalness:** This is non-negotiable. The delivery must be smooth, the enunciation crisp, the pacing natural, and free of any noticeable digital artifacts or the "hiss" of older TTS systems. High-fidelity voices should handle complex terminology, diverse sentence structures, and challenging proper nouns in a way that is virtually indistinguishable from a professional human reader.

- **Accent, Dialect, and Regional Characteristics:** The accent (e.g., General American, RP British, Australian, Scottish) must intentionally complement the podcast's topic and resonate authentically with the target demographic. A thematic mismatch—such as a formal British accent for a deeply casual American pop culture review—creates immediate cognitive dissonance. Different accents carry specific connotations (e.g., authoritative, academic, friendly, street-smart) that must be strategically aligned with the desired tone.
- **Demonstrated Emotional Range:** For any narrative, documentary, or emotionally resonant content, the voice must convincingly convey the required affect. The creator should rigorously test voices using emotionally demanding script passages. The platform's ability to interpret or allow explicit emotional cues is a major differentiating factor.
- **Theme and Tone Alignment:** The voice should feel like an organic extension of the content's central purpose. A podcast dedicated to serious, investigative historical analysis demands an authoritative, measured, and perhaps lower-pitched voice, while a dynamic, fast-paced comedy podcast would be better served by an energetic, approachable, and higher-cadence voice.
- **Advanced Customization Features (Granularity of Control):** The best platforms offer granular, non-destructive control over essential vocal parameters. This includes **Speaking Speed (Rate)** for pacing, **Pitch** for character or host differentiation, **Volume** for emphasis, sophisticated **Emotional Style** settings, and the precise insertion of **Pauses (Breaths)** and **Emphasis (Stress)** on specific words. This level of control is essential for crafting genuinely unique and complex vocal profiles.

III. Advanced Customization: Voice Cloning and Bespoke Voice Creation

AI technology extends far beyond pre-recorded libraries, granting creators unprecedented control over their podcast's singular sonic identity.

AI Voice Cloning (The Digital Twin):

This sophisticated process involves training a specialized neural network on an extensive, high-quality audio dataset of a single individual's voice. The AI meticulously learns the unique pitch signature, vocal timbre, characteristic cadence, and subtle, often subconscious, inflections that define that person's speaking pattern. The result is a generative model that can synthesize *any* new text input in a voice that is a near-perfect digital replica of the original human.

- **Application:** The primary use is maintaining absolute **brand consistency**. If a signature host is unavailable, ill, or needs to rapidly produce supplementary content, their cloned voice ensures a consistent, high-quality listening experience across all episodes and projects. It is also used to ensure recurring characters in audio fiction maintain a perfectly consistent vocal presence.
- **Ethical and Legal Imperative: Explicit, fully informed, and documented consent** from the individual being cloned is not merely a courtesy—it is an absolute legal and ethical necessity. Reputable AI platforms enforce rigorous security protocols and verification steps to prevent fraudulent use, unauthorized impersonation, or 'deep-fake' misuse.

Custom Voice Creation (Engineering a New Persona):

Rather than replicating an existing human, custom voice creation involves constructing a wholly novel vocal profile. This can be done by building the voice from the ground up or through extensive, heavy modification of an existing base model. Creators can define specific, interlocking parameters for perceived **age**, **gender**, **vocal weight/projection**, levels of **breathiness**, and general **personality traits** (e.g., "warm and reassuring" or "cold and metallic") to engineer a unique, trademark voice for their show.

- **Application:** Creating distinct, memorable podcast **personas** that embody the show's theme. Examples include a futuristic, clean, emotionless AI voice for a highly technical podcast; a gritty, historical-sounding voice for a true crime show; or an empathetic, calming voice designed specifically for sensitive or therapeutic content.

IV. Integrating AI Voices into the Professional Production Workflow

Successful integration of AI voices demands a strategic, multi-phase approach encompassing script preparation, audio generation, and professional post-production.

Phase 1: The Script Preparation and Markup Phase:

1. **Clean, Optimized Script:** Ensure impeccable punctuation. Use commas, dashes, and periods strategically to guide the AI's natural pause and pacing structure. Numerals and symbols should be written out (e.g., "twenty-five percent" instead of "25%") if the AI struggles with shorthand forms.
2. **Explicit Pronunciation Guides:** For difficult jargon, unique proper nouns, company names, or foreign words, embed pho-

netic spellings or utilization of the platform's custom dictionary feature. This pre-empts costly re-renders.

3. **Logical Segmentation:** Break the master script into smaller, contextually manageable chunks (e.g., by paragraph or scene change). This facilitates easier generation, error correction, and subsequent editing/rearrangement.

Phase 2: Generation and Fine-Tuning Configuration:

1. **Voice and Parameter Selection:** Select the chosen AI voice and rigorously fine-tune the parameters (Speed, Pitch, Emotional Tone) to ensure consistency with the established host or character persona.
2. **Strategic Pacing and Emphasis:** Utilize the platform's features for inserting intentional pauses (breaths) and applying specific emphasis (stress) to key words, which is crucial for mimicking the nuances of natural human rhetorical delivery.
3. **High-Fidelity Export:** Generate the final audio and download it in the highest quality format supported (e.g., lossless WAV files are preferred over compressed MP3 for post-production).

Phase 3: The Editing and Mixing Phase (Digital Audio Workstation - DAW):

The raw AI audio must be expertly integrated with all other sonic elements—music, sound effects, and human speech—to achieve a professional master.

- **Volume and Level Consistency:** Ensure the AI voice is consistently placed in the mix's volume range. Use **volume automation** throughout the track for subtle, non-destructive adjustments to dynamics.

- **EQ (Equalization) for Clarity and Warmth:** Apply corrective and enhancement EQ. Often, AI voices can sound slightly thin or overly "sibilant" (too much 'S' sound). Use EQ to gently roll off harsh high frequencies and boost the mid-low frequencies to "warm up" the sound and give it more human-like presence.
- **Compression for Dynamic Control:** Apply moderate, transparent compression to smooth out the dynamic range, ensuring the delivery is consistent across the entire episode without unnatural volume spikes or dips.
- **Rhythmic Pacing and Flow:** Pay meticulous attention to the transitions *between* AI segments and with other audio. Use subtle **crossfades** or musical stings to ensure a fluid, natural rhythm that avoids jarring cuts.
- **Sonic Cohesion (When Mixing AI and Human Voices):** If the podcast features both AI and human narration, apply a near-identical chain of EQ, compression, and reverb (if used) settings to both sets of tracks. This "glues" the sounds together, maintaining a single, cohesive sonic profile.
- **Background Music Ducking:** Automate the background music or sound effects to **duck** (temporarily and smoothly lower in volume) the instant the AI voice begins speaking, ensuring maximal vocal clarity and avoiding a cluttered mix.

V. Ethical Considerations and Managing Listener Perception

In the rapidly evolving landscape of AI-generated content, transparency and managing audience expectations are paramount for building and maintaining the trust that is the bedrock of any successful podcast.

The Imperative of Transparency and Disclosure:

- **Explicit Disclosure is Mandatory (Informational Content):** For non-fiction, informational, documentary, or news-based podcasts, explicitly stating the use of AI voices is not optional. This disclosure should be prominent (e.g., in the intro, outro, show notes, or a dedicated segment). Failure to disclose, when the content is presented as factual human narration, can lead to accusations of deception and a catastrophic erosion of listener trust.
- **Contextual Disclosure (Fictional Content):** In audio dramas or fictional podcasts where the primary goal is narrative immersion, disclosure can be more subtle (e.g., listed in the credits or the technical notes). However, disclosure should still be provided to respect the audience's curiosity about the creative process and the true source of the voices.

Managing and Optimizing Listener Perception:

- **Quality Above All:** A robotic, monotonous, or poorly mixed AI voice will inevitably lead to a negative audience perception, regardless of disclosure. Meticulous selection, advanced fine-tuning, and professional editing are the most crucial safeguards against listener alienation.
- **Enhance the Narrative, Do Not Detract:** The AI voice must serve the content and the narrative structure. Creators must leverage the advanced emotional expression capabilities to make the delivery engaging, not simply functional.
- **Strategic and Focused Use:** If concerns about the "humanity" or emotional connection of the podcast exist, use AI voices for clearly defined, specialized segments (e.g., summarizing research, reading a fictional text quote, or supporting roles) while retaining authentic human voices for the core hosting, personal commentary, and emotional connections.

- **Authenticity of Underlying Content:** The delivery mechanism should not overshadow the message. Ensure the underlying script is rich with human perspective, genuine insight, and compelling storytelling. A strong narrative transcends the technical delivery method.
- **Broader Ethical Responsibility (Fact-Checking):** The ease with which complex, believable narratives can be generated with AI places an even greater ethical obligation on the creator to rigorously fact-check and verify all information, especially for news, educational, or highly sensitive content, to prevent the proliferation of convincing misinformation.

The integration of AI voices is not a compromise; it is a powerful, sophisticated enhancement to the modern podcaster's toolkit, offering unparalleled creative control and efficiency. By proactively embracing transparency, rigorously prioritizing a high-quality audio experience, and thoughtfully integrating the technology, creators can successfully harness this revolution to produce richer, more accessible, and profoundly innovative audio content for the next generation of listeners.

10

Designing Professional Cover Art with AI

In the fiercely contested, exponentially growing digital domain of podcasting, which today hosts millions of distinct shows and generates billions of downloads annually, the success of a show hinges on a single, fleeting moment of connection. The podcast cover art transcends the definition of a mere visual accessory; it is, unequivocally, the most critical visual element, functioning as the show's crucial first impression, its immediate digital handshake with a potential listener, and the single greatest factor influencing the decision to click "play" or scroll past. This strategic image is positioned as the primary visual asset across the globe's high-traffic directories—Apple Podcasts, Spotify, Google Podcasts, Amazon Music, and Stitcher. It acts as the ultimate gatekeeper to the meticulously researched, recorded, and edited audio content within. Without a visually compelling, immediately professional, and strategically designed hook, even the most insightful, thrilling, or niche show is destined to remain undiscovered, hopelessly lost within the dense algorithmic noise and overwhelming competition.

The profound commercial and psychological significance of cover art mirrors that of foundational media assets—the captivating book jacket, the genre-defining movie poster, or the iconic album cover. It is the initial artifact that ignites the imagination, unequivocally hints at the show's genre, and decisively establishes the overall tone and the perceived quality expectation. Given the sheer, paralyzing volume of available podcasts, the cover art instantly becomes the primary differentiator, broadcasting a critical signal of professionalism, production quality, and immediate relevance. Amateurish, generic, or uninspired cover art suggests a profound lack of effort, investment, or editorial rigor, leading discerning listeners to naturally and logically assume the audio content is similarly lacking. Conversely, strong, sophisticated, and well-executed visual appeal is scientifically proven to significantly boost the all-important click-through rates (CTR) across every digital content platform, and podcasts are absolutely no exception. An attractive, relevant, and exquisitely composed image is the first, essential hurdle in subscriber acquisition, powerfully reinforcing perceived quality and setting positive, high expectations for the immersive listening experience that follows.

Beyond the initial barrier of discoverability, cover art is the foundational pillar upon which the entire show's brand identity is built. It serves as the consistent visual anchor connecting and unifying all promotional and marketing efforts, from targeted social media advertisements and channel headers to website banners, email signatures, and even merchandise. A distinctive, memorable, and visually unique piece of cover art builds instant recognition, systematically fostering listener trust and enduring loyalty. It functions as the visual signature that listeners immediately and permanently associate with the show's unique value proposition, the host personalities, and its core message. This strong visual brand fosters crucial familiarity, encouraging not only continued listening and subscription retention but also organic word-of-mouth recommendations, which ultimately transform casual listeners into enthusiastic, loyal, and vocal brand advocates.

Core Principles of Compelling Cover Art Design: Attract, Inform, and Engage

To engineer truly effective cover art that possesses the necessary visual authority to cut through the digital noise, several fundamental design principles must be meticulously applied in absolute synergy to attract the eye, inform the potential listener, and ultimately engage the precise target audience:1. Clarity and Readability: The Absolute Thumbnail Test

The defining constraint of podcast cover art is its primary display environment: the thumbnail.

- **Legibility at Scale is Paramount:** Since cover art is predominantly viewed at tiny thumbnail sizes—often no larger than a postage stamp on a mobile phone screen—the podcast title and any essential branding elements must be instantly, effortlessly readable. Designers must rigorously avoid overly intricate script fonts, excessively small type sizes, or the debilitating use of too much text, all of which instantly dissolve into an unreadable visual mash at scale.
- **Optimal Font Choice and Contrast:** The typography must be a deliberate, conscious extension of the podcast's inherent identity and tone—for example, a formal, historical serif font for a serious history or literature review show, or a playful, clean sans-serif for a conversational comedy or personal development show. The title should be concise, utilize bold or heavy weighting for maximum presence, and stand out with extreme contrast against the background elements (e.g., pure white text on a solid dark color).

2. Relevance to Content and Tone: Providing Visual Context

The artwork should be a direct, non-verbal communication of the show's subject matter.

- **The Immediate Visual Hint:** The artwork must offer a direct, symbolic, or representative visual clue about the podcast's core subject matter and the overall emotional mood. Technology and business podcasts might leverage digital patterns, clean geometric lines, or abstract data visualizations; true-crime and mystery shows benefit from dark tones, stark imagery, or minimalist, ominous iconography; and comedy should generally employ bright, vibrant color palettes, exaggerated graphics, or light-hearted, expressive characters.
- **Efficient Audience Self-Selection:** This immediate and clear visual connection serves a critical dual purpose: it efficiently draws in listeners who are genuinely interested in the topic while simultaneously deterring those who are not. This organic process of self-selection leads to a more engaged, higher-retention core audience, reducing vanity metrics.

3. Originality and Memorability: The Imperative to Stand Out

In a crowded marketplace, generic visuals are invisible.

- **Avoid the Cliché Trap:** Relying on generic, low-effort stock photos or industry-specific clichés (the ubiquitous, boring image of a microphone or headphones) fails entirely to capture attention or signal uniqueness. A necessary investment in success involves commissioning custom design, procuring unique illustrations, or leveraging advanced generative AI tools to create a unique, eye-catching, and instantly recognizable visual brand mark. The ultimate goal is a visual asset that is unique enough to be instantly recallable from a lineup of similar shows.

4. Technical Considerations: Directory Compliance is Non-Negotiable

Flawless execution requires adherence to universal technical standards.

- **Format and Dimensions:** Cover art must strictly adhere to industry technical guidelines to ensure maximum compatibility and optimal display quality across all platforms. It must be a perfect square image, with a minimum required resolution of **1400x1400 pixels** and a maximum resolution of **3000x3000 pixels**. The final file should be saved in either a high-quality **JPEG** or transparent **PNG** format, using the RGB color space. Adhering to these universal industry standards is non-negotiable for seamless acceptance and crisp, pixel-perfect display across all major podcast directories.

Foundational Design Elements for Impact: The Designer's Toolkit Applied

The foundation of striking cover art lies in the thoughtful, skilled application of fundamental design principles, treating the square canvas not as a limitation, but as a miniature, high-impact poster:

Composition: The Art of Arrangement and Focus

Composition dictates the intentional arrangement of all visual elements to create a harmonious, balanced, and impactful visual statement.

- **Clear Focal Point:** Every truly successful design requires a single, clear focal point—the element that first and most strongly draws the viewer's eye (typically the title or a distinctive graphic element). All other elements should be intentionally placed to support and frame this anchor.

- **The Rule of Thirds:** Instead of relying on static, centered arrangements, placing key elements along the imaginary lines or at the intersections of a 3x3 grid often creates a more dynamic, energetic, and visually interesting image that naturally guides the viewer's eye.
- **The Power of Negative Space:** Intentional and strategic utilization of empty space (also known as white space) is crucial. It helps isolate and emphasize the focal point, prevents the design from becoming cluttered, overwhelming, or busy, and significantly increases overall readability and perceived visual sophistication.

Color Theory: Psychology, Contrast, and Emotion

Color is one of the most powerful non-verbal communicators available to the designer.

- **Psychological Impact:** Colors evoke specific emotions, cultural associations, and immediate feelings. The chosen color palette must be meticulously and consciously aligned with the podcast's theme, content, and emotional tone.
- **Essential Contrast:** High contrast between text and the background is absolutely non-negotiable for maximum legibility, especially at small sizes (e.g., bright white or vibrant yellow text on a deep black or dark colored background).
- **Emotional Messaging:** Warm color palettes (reds, oranges, yellows) are typically used to suggest energy, passion, urgency, or excitement; conversely, cool colors (blues, greens, purples) convey calmness, trust, reliability, mystery, or introspection. The satura-

tion and brightness of the colors further impact the overall mood and visual punch.

Typography: The Show's Silent Voice

The font choice sets the intellectual and emotional stage for the show's content.

- **Prioritizing Readability:** The chosen font acts as the "silent voice" of the show. It must be instantly legible and easily differentiated at the smallest thumbnail size.
- **Intentional Typeface Choice: Serif fonts** (with small finishing strokes) often convey a sense of tradition, authority, and sophistication (ideal for history, literature, or academic podcasts). **Sans-serif fonts** (without finishing strokes) are modern, clean, and direct (versatile for news, technology, and contemporary topics). Highly decorative, handwritten, or script fonts should be universally avoided, as they quickly become illegible when scaled down.
- **Establishing Hierarchy:** Use a strict maximum of one or two complementary fonts. Ensure the size and weight of the main title are substantial (bold or heavy) and that there is proper micro-spacing (kerning and tracking) to maximize clarity.

Imagery: Building the Visual Narrative

The visual elements must tell a story or symbolize a core concept.

- **Direct Relevance:** All visual elements, whether high-quality photographs, bespoke illustrations, or abstract graphics, must directly or indirectly relate to the podcast's subject matter and tone.

The use of high-quality, sharp, and well-lit imagery is a non-negotiable sign of professional production value.

- **Symbolism Over Literalism:** To add intellectual depth and intriguing memorability, utilize symbolic representations (e.g., a lightning bolt for a sudden idea, a mountain for overcoming a challenge, a compass for direction) rather than overly literal, descriptive depictions.
- **Style Consistency:** The artistic style employed (e.g., photorealistic, impressionistic, watercolor, vector art, flat design) must be rigorously consistent with the show's overall aesthetic tone and carefully tailored to the visual preferences of the target audience.

Leveraging Generative AI for Next-Generation Cover Art Creation and Refinement

The recent, rapid, and profound rise of generative AI image platforms (such as Midjourney, DALL-E 3, Adobe Firefly, and Stable Diffusion) has fundamentally democratized the creation of professional-grade cover art, making high-quality, unique visuals accessible to even the most independent, budget-conscious podcasters. These powerful tools flawlessly translate complex textual prompts into unique, sophisticated visual art, effectively shifting the necessary focus from technical mastery of complicated design software to imaginative direction and precise creative communication.The Art of Prompt Engineering for Superior Visual Output

The success and quality of AI-generated results are entirely dependent on crafting highly detailed, clear, and multi-faceted prompts that precisely guide the AI's complex creative engine. A truly strong and effective prompt should systematically include the following seven layers of critical instruction:

1. **Subject Matter:** The core thematic concept or object (e.g., "a futuristic robotic archaeologist excavating ancient ruins on Mars").
2. **Style and Medium:** The desired aesthetic quality and artistic rendering (e.g., "hyperrealistic photography," "Art Deco illustration," "a watercolor painting in the style of Van Gogh," "minimalist vector art").
3. **Mood and Atmosphere:** The emotional tone the image must convey (e.g., "serene and contemplative," "playful and energetic," "dark, cinematic, and ominous").
4. **Color Palette:** Specific required colors or schemes (e.g., "a limited palette of cool blues and purples," "vibrant neons with high contrast," "muted earth tones and gold accents").
5. **Composition and Framing:** The desired arrangement of elements and camera perspective (e.g., "centered subject with a wide lens view," "close-up portrait shot," "dynamic diagonal composition").
6. **Lighting:** The specific quality and direction of light (e.g., "dramatic chiaroscuro lighting," "soft diffused light from a window," "neon street light glow," "studio ring light").
7. **Essential Keywords:** Practical platform-specific terms that optimize the output for the required format, such as "podcast cover art," "square aspect ratio," or "suitable for text overlay."

Example Prompt Progression for a Theoretical Science Podcast ("The Cosmic Query"):

- *Initial (Too generic, poor result):* "Space podcast cover art." (Result: Likely a generic, low-effort, unoriginal stock star photo.)
- *Refined (Specific and successful, high-impact result):* "A breathtaking, hyperrealistic image of a swirling nebula in deep space, featuring vibrant blues, purples, and striking hints of gold. Include a lone, highly detailed silhouetted spacecraft visible in the

distance, suggesting deep exploration. Render this in a dark, cinematic tone, suitable for a science podcast cover art with a square aspect ratio. Add atmospheric volumetric lighting for depth and drama, 3000x3000 resolution."

Post-Generation Refinement with Advanced AI Tools

Even after the initial generation, AI tools remain invaluable for meticulously refining and perfecting the visual assets, moving beyond initial creation into the realm of professional polish:

- **AI Upscaling and Sharpening:** These sophisticated tools intelligently increase the image resolution (e.g., from a standard 1024x1024 to the maximum required 3000x3000 pixels) without introducing noticeable pixelation. They use complex algorithms to intelligently add realistic detail and sharpness for a crisp, high-end professional look that reads well on Retina displays.
- **Background Removal and Compositing:** AI can accurately isolate the main subject from a busy background with pixel-perfect precision, allowing for flexible compositing onto a new, more thematic or simplified backdrop. This is critical for achieving brand consistency across different promotional materials.
- **Color Correction and Enhancement:** Advanced AI can analyze and automatically adjust the color balance, vibrancy, saturation, and temperature of the image, ensuring the final color palette precisely matches the intended mood and brand guidelines without manual, time-consuming adjustments.
- **Generative Fill and Content-Aware Editing:** The most advanced tools allow users to seamlessly extend the canvas (to better accommodate a large title) or to modify, remove, or replace specific elements within the image (e.g., changing the color of an

object, removing a distracting shadow), offering ultimate compositional control and post-production flexibility.

By strategically integrating generative AI for both initial creation and detailed refinement, podcasters can efficiently achieve high-quality, professional cover art that serves as a powerful, tireless, and silent ambassador for their show in the hyper-competitive digital space.

11

Choosing a Hosting Platform and Distribution

The RSS (Really Simple Syndication) feed stands as the foundational technical engine that drives the entire, decentralized podcasting world. Far from being a mere technicality, this specialized file is the invisible, yet **absolutely essential** bridge connecting your meticulously crafted audio files, securely stored on your hosting platform, to the vast, fragmented, and global ecosystem of listening apps and directories. Without this standardized digital blueprint, your podcast cannot be discovered, consumed, or measured, making it the single most important component in the distribution chain.Deconstructing the RSS Feed: A Dynamic XML Blueprint

At its core, the RSS feed is a specialized, human-readable text file, almost universally formatted in the XML (Extensible Markup Language) standard. This file serves as the singular, dynamic blueprint for your entire podcast show. It is not static; rather, it is continuously updated by your host and constantly "checked" or "crawled" by every listening platform—often multiple times per hour—to ensure content freshness.

This critical file houses all the crucial, structured metadata about your show, meticulously categorized using strict industry tags and schemas (often defined by dominant players like Apple Podcasts) to ensure universal compatibility and proper rendering across diverse applications and devices.Channel-Level Metadata (The Show Itself)

This segment includes the overarching, permanent details that define your brand and show to both potential listeners and the search algorithms of directories.

- **Podcast Title & Subtitle:** How your show is named and briefly described. This is critical for initial discoverability and establishing your unique selling proposition.
- **Show Description (Summary):** The long-form text that outlines your podcast's purpose, content themes, and host information. This is a vital area for incorporating keywords to improve SEO (Search Engine Optimization) within the directory ecosystem.
- **Cover Artwork URL:** The specific, high-resolution, permanent link to your square artwork (mandated dimensions typically range from 1400x1400 to 3000x3000 pixels). This visual element is the primary brand identifier in every app.
- **Categories and Subcategories:** The designated industry tags (e.g., *Technology > Gadgets*, *Arts > Design*) that help directories categorize your content. These are crucial for placement in browsing sections and can significantly impact organic discovery.
- **Author and Owner Contact Information:** Critical for copyright and directory management. The owner's email address is used for verification and communication with directories.
- **Language and Explicit Tagging:** Key flags that inform directories about the content's spoken language (e.g., <language>en-us</language>) and its maturity level (<itunes:explicit>yes/no</itunes:explicit>). Proper tagging ensures compliance with app store policies.

Item-Level Metadata (Individual Episodes)

For every single episode you have ever published, the feed contains a dedicated <item> block. This structure allows directories to display chronological episode information.

- **Episode Title, Description (Show Notes), and Publication Date:** Contextual information for listeners and algorithms. The show notes are where listeners find links and references mentioned in the episode.
- **Direct Audio Links (The Enclosure Tag):** Most importantly, the <enclosure> tag provides the **specific, permanent URLs pointing directly to the MP3 or AAC audio files** for each episode stored on your host's servers. This is the exact mechanism that allows listening apps to initiate the streaming or download process. **The directories never touch the audio file itself.**
- **Episode Duration and File Size:** Technical metrics (e.g., <itunes:duration>) used by the listener app to display playback length and manage downloads.
- **Season and Episode Numbering:** Structured tags (<itunes:season>, <itunes:episode>) that allow for accurate sorting and display of serialized or seasonal content.

The Dynamics of Decentralized Distribution: A 'Publish Once, Distribute Everywhere' Engine

The true power of the RSS feed lies in its **dynamic and standardized nature**, enabling the core principle of podcasting: publishing once and distributing everywhere without requiring individual uploads to dozens of platforms.

1. **The Hosting Hub:** When you upload a new episode to your podcast hosting service (e.g., Libsyn, Buzzsprout, Anchor), the

host performs two crucial, simultaneous actions: a) it stores the audio file on its high-speed, global Content Delivery Network (CDN), and b) it **automatically updates the XML feed file**, inserting a new <item> tag that contains all the episode data and the new, direct audio link.

2. **Directories as Persistent Readers:** Podcast directories (like Apple Podcasts, Spotify, Amazon Music, and Google Podcasts) **do not host your audio files** or the RSS file itself. Instead, they operate as powerful, automated "RSS readers" or "crawlers." They are programmed to periodically and frequently "check" (or "crawl") the unique, permanent URL of your RSS feed for any changes or new entries.
3. **Automatic Syndication and Synchronization:** When a directory's crawler detects a new entry or a modification in your feed, it instantly pulls the updated metadata. This information is then processed and made available to its millions of users. This automated, standardized process ensures that a single upload to your host is near-instantaneously synchronized across every listening platform where your feed is registered, creating a unified and efficient distribution network.

The Role of the RSS Feed: The Definitive Source of Truth

The RSS feed is not merely a pipeline; it is the **definitive, canonical source of truth** for your entire podcast. Its integrity and content directly govern your show's performance, discoverability, and accessibility. Any inconsistency or error in the feed ripples across the entire distribution network.

- **Gateway to Directories:** When you first submit your show to any major directory, you are not uploading files; you are simply providing the permanent URL of this feed. From that point forward, the directory relies *only* on that URL for all future updates, show changes, and episode releases. If you change hosts, you must manage a 301 redirect within the original feed.

- **Discoverability and SEO:** Directory and app algorithms heavily rely on the structured information contained within your RSS feed (titles, show descriptions, episode descriptions, categories) to match your content with listener searches. A well-structured, keyword-rich feed is **paramount for being found** in a saturated market. The metadata in the feed acts as your podcast's primary SEO (Search Engine Optimization) strategy.
- **Universal, Open Standard:** The RSS format is standardized according to specifications set by organizations like Apple and industry bodies. This standardization is what allows a single feed to power your presence across a multitude of different listening applications (from smartphone apps to smart speakers and car dashboards), ensuring the decentralized, open, and platform-agnostic nature that defines modern podcasting.
- **Monetization Hooks and Analytics:** Modern podcasting features, including dynamic ad insertion platforms (which personalize ads to individual listeners) and advanced analytics tools (which track downloads and listening behavior), operate by reading the RSS feed. They use specific tags within the feed (like <podcast:location> or <podcast:funding>) to understand where to insert advertisements or to attribute download requests, adding another critical layer of reliance on the feed's structure.

Troubleshooting and Management: The Diagnostics Center

Your podcast hosting provider is entirely responsible for generating, hosting, and maintaining an industry-compliant, well-formatted RSS feed. They provide you with the unique, persistent URL in your dashboard. If distribution issues arise, the RSS feed URL and its contents are the first and only place to look for diagnostics:

Issue	Common RSS Feed Cause	Resolution A
New episode not appearing on directories	Incorrectly formatted episode data (e.g., missing required metadata like a title, date, or explicit tag). The directory's crawler encountered an error and skipped the update.	Validate the X using an industry validator tool. Ch dashboard for pu or incomplete fiel
Playback error or slow loading	A broken, expired, or inaccessible URL for the audio file (<enclosure>) within the feed, or the audio file's hosting server is experiencing a network outage.	Confirm the a correct and resolv Check the host's page for network
Incorrect artwork, show title, or category	A necessary update (e.g., new artwork) has been made on the host but has not yet been "pulled" by the directory from the updated feed due to a delayed crawl cycle.	In the case of sues, refresh the f within the directo sion portal (e.g., A casts Connect) or for the next sched which can take up
Missing episodes or truncated feed	The feed has exceeded a platform's historical episode limit, or the hosting platform has misconfigured the feed's history settings, sometimes unintentionally omitting old episodes.	Verify the hos limits and ensure are marked as "pu included in the pu tings.

In essence, the RSS feed is the technological linchpin that allows a single voice and a single file upload to reach a global audience with remarkable efficiency, defining the very architecture of podcast distribution. Understanding its function is not just a technical exercise; it is key to mastering the distribution, sustained growth, and maintenance of your podcast.

12

Marketing Your Podcast and Growing Your Audience

The launch of a podcast is merely the starting line. The true race for listener attention and sustained growth hinges on a **dynamic, well-thought-out marketing strategy**. Far beyond the technical setup and episode creation, proactive marketing is the indispensable engine that ensures your voice breaks through the immense digital noise and resonates with its intended, high-value audience. A passive approach guarantees invisibility; therefore, the marketing effort must be a continuous, evolving cycle focused on cultivating, connecting with, and growing your podcast's presence across all relevant platforms and listener touchpoints. This is not a task to be delegated to the occasional social media post but a core business function.Phase I: Establishing the Unshakeable Foundation: Strategy and Audience Mastery

A strong marketing edifice requires more than just good intentions; it demands clear, quantifiable goals and an intimate, almost empathetic understanding of the people you aim to serve. This foundation minimizes wasted effort and maximizes return on investment (time and capital).1. Defining Success with SMART Goals: The Marketing Compass

The pursuit of "more listeners" is a strategy destined for drift. Success in podcasting must be concretely defined using the **Specific, Measurable, Achievable, Relevant, and Time-bound (SMART)** framework.

These objectives are the compass and roadmap for your marketing journey, providing direction, a mechanism for progress tracking, and the justification for strategic adjustments. They transform abstract desires into actionable projects.

Goal Type	Vague Example	SMART Example	Strategic Function	fo
Growth	Get more downloads.	Increase weekly downloads by 15% within the next quarter (Q3 2026).	Measures marketing efficacy, audience reach expansion, and channel performance.	loa scr Do ity tin
Engagement	Have listeners talk about the show.	Gain 500 new reviews/ratings on Apple Podcasts and Spotify by the end of the year.	Validates content quality, acts as powerful social proof, and improves directory ranking algorithms.	Co Ra M Co un
Monetization	Make money from the show.	Secure two sponsorship deals at a minimum $500 CPM rate within six months.	Aligns marketing efforts with business outcomes and provides runway for production quality improvements.	Re Co Cl A

Community	Build a dedicated audience.	Grow the private Facebook Group by 250 highly-engaged members this quarter with an average of 3 posts per member per week.	Tracks depth of connection, listener loyalty, and the potential for organic, word-of-mouth marketing.	C bersh Com quen Resp

Crucially, all SMART goals must maintain an unwavering alignment with the podcast's overarching mission, whether that mission is establishing thought leadership, building a community, driving specific business traffic, or supporting a personal brand.2. Deep Dive: Intimate Audience Understanding (The Listener Persona)

Effective marketing is impossible without a granular understanding of the person on the other end of the headphones. Developing a detailed **listener persona** moves beyond simple demographics to deep psychographics, revealing the core of *why* they listen, what motivates them, their consumption habits, and their most pressing pain points.

- **Demographics:** Age range, gender identity, geographical location, income bracket, educational background, marital status.
- **Professional Background (if applicable):** Industry, specific job title, career goals, professional challenges.
- **Psychographics:** Hobbies, values, core beliefs, media consumption patterns, and, most importantly, **why they listen** (e.g., entertainment, continuous learning/professional development, seeking community, need for background comfort, inspiration).
- **Media Consumption Habits:** What other podcasts and content creators do they follow? Which social media platforms do they frequent, and at what times of day? When do they typically

listen to podcasts (e.g., commute, workout, chores, dedicated listening time)? *This informs release times and promotional platform focus.*

This level of detail allows you to tailor your content, messaging (the copy used in ads and show notes), and promotional channel selection for maximum resonance. This deep dive is not a one-time exercise; it is an **ongoing process**, continually refined using new data from hosting analytics, direct audience surveys, and social listening.Phase II: The Backbone of Promotion: The Integrated PESO Model

A truly cohesive marketing strategy employs a synergistic approach by integrating three key categories of promotional channels, ensuring they collectively amplify your podcast's reach and authority.

Channel Category	Definition	Key Assets	Str and B
1. Owned Media	Channels and platforms you directly control, giving you full command over content and distribution.	Podcast Website (SEO-Optimized), Email List (The Superfan Channel), Branded Social Profiles (as distribution tools).	Th provid manen against change direct nicatio
2. Earned Media	Publicity gained through third-party endorsement or organic sharing, leveraging external credibility.	Guest appearances (on other shows/media), Media Mentions, High-quality Reviews, Word-of-Mouth (WOM) referrals.	Th form c leverag and cr resulti qualifi

3. Paid Media	Strategic advertising investment used to accelerate growth and target precise listener segments.	Targeted Social Media Ads (Facebook, Instagram, LinkedIn), Podcast Advertising Networks, SEM (Google Ads), Sponsored Content/Shout-outs.	Used reach exp ing new precisely niche de that are c reach org

Phase III: Tactical Implementation: Consistency, Discoverability, and Automation

Successful execution is characterized by unwavering **consistency**—in publishing high-quality episodes and maintaining a reliable, value-driven presence on chosen promotional channels. Sporadic marketing yields sporadic, unsustainable results.A. Search Engine Optimization (SEO) and AI for Superior Discoverability

SEO is the fundamental process of making your content understandable and visible to search engines (Google, Bing) and, crucially, to internal podcast directory search engines (Spotify, Apple Podcasts, etc.). This is how passive, sustained growth is achieved.

1. **Optimize Foundational Elements:** Use clear, compelling, **keyword-rich language** in your **podcast title, subtitle, and overall show description** within the RSS feed and directories. These fields are high-value real estate that algorithms use to categorize and surface your show.
2. **Detailed Show Notes as Rank Magnets:** Every episode is a dedicated web page opportunity. Show notes must be **detailed, well-structured (with headers and bullet points), and rich with relevant keywords and concepts** discussed in the episode.

They serve as the crawlable text that search engines index to understand your content's topic depth.

3. **The SEO Powerhouse: Full Transcripts:** Providing **full, accurate transcripts** on your website is arguably the single most effective SEO tool for a podcast. Transcripts create vast amounts of indexable text content, making your episodes discoverable for highly specific, long-tail search queries and simultaneously catering to critical accessibility needs.
4. **Leveraging AI for SEO Superiority and Efficiency:**

    - **Keyword Research:** AI tools rapidly identify trending topics, analyze search intent, and pinpoint both high-volume and valuable long-tail keywords relevant to your niche. This takes the guesswork out of topic selection.
    - **Content Optimization:** AI suggests real-time improvements for clarity, flow, and optimal keyword density in your episode descriptions and show notes before publishing.
    - **Transcription:** Providing accurate, efficient, and affordable audio-to-text conversion is a major time-saver, often integrating directly with editing workflows.
    - **Audience Analysis:** AI can analyze search queries leading to your site and directory performance to refine your content strategy based on what is actively resonating with the search landscape, creating a data-driven content feedback loop.

B. Strategic Social Media Marketing: Moving Beyond the Link Drop

Social media must move beyond simply broadcasting episode links. It requires creating engaging, platform-specific content that *earns* attention, builds a community, and provides standalone value. Repurposing audio into visual formats is paramount.

Platform	Core Strategy	Key Tactics (Native)
Instagram (Visual/Short-Form)	Humanize the show; create desire through captivating visuals and soundbites.	**Audiograms** dio clips), **Reels** v highlights and cap hind-the-scenes st branded/niche ha the Link-in-Bio tc
Twitter / X (Conversational)	Focus on quick engagement and real-time discussion around episode topics and current events.	Concise messa ing down episode **Twitter threads** cro-blogging), hos **Spaces** for audien
Facebook (Community & Nurture)	Nurture a dedicated, deeply engaged community away from the public feed.	Leverage **Facel** for exclusive Q&A cussions, polls, an tent; use interacti quizzes.
LinkedIn (Professional)	Demonstrate expertise, establish thought leadership, and target B2B/professional listeners.	Share in-depth articles and insigh from episodes; use for professional su key takeaways.
TikTok (Short-form Video)	Capture attention and leverage viral trends through highly engaging, easily digestible clips.	Create quick, grabbing hooks, h skits, or animated tied to episode top native trends and

C. Email Marketing: The Superfan Channel and Owned Asset

The email list is your most invaluable asset—a direct, intimate channel for nurturing your most dedicated listeners, bypassing the volatility and control of social media algorithms. This is your insurance policy against platform changes.

1. **High-Value Acquisition via Lead Magnets:** Offer a **compelling, valuable asset** that perfectly aligns with your podcast's content (e.g., a checklist, a bonus episode, a comprehensive guide, a private Q&A session) in exchange for an email address. The value must clearly outweigh the cost of giving personal data.
2. **Consistent, Value-Driven Newsletters:** Newsletters must offer more than mere episode announcements. They should provide:
    - **Episode Recaps with Deeper Dives** and personal reflections from the host.
    - **Behind-the-Scenes Content** and host insights to foster an "inner circle" feeling.
    - **Exclusive Q&A Segments** or early access to bonus content.
    - **Curated Resources** (links, articles, books) to position the host as a knowledgeable curator.
    - **Clear Calls to Action (CTAs)** guiding listeners to listen, review, or join the community.
3. **Segmentation:** Target communication based on listener preferences (e.g., topic interest via survey) or engagement levels (e.g., open rate) to ensure maximum relevance and open rates, preventing list fatigue.
4. **Compelling Subject Lines:** Use concise, intriguing, and benefit-oriented language to boost open rates and reduce unsubscribes. Avoid spam triggers.

D. Cross-Promotion and Strategic Collaboration: Audience Injection

Effectively leverage the audiences of other established podcasts and creators to jump-start growth and achieve massive, targeted visibility. This relies on the principle of complementary audiences.

- **Guesting on Other Podcasts (The "Halo" Effect):** This is a direct injection into a relevant, engaged listener base. Listeners of other podcasts are already accustomed to the medium, making them highly qualified leads.
    - **Identify Aligned Shows:** Look for podcasts with a similar or complementary target audience, avoiding direct competitors unless collaboration is the goal. Focus on shows slightly larger than yours for maximum impact.
    - **Craft a Compelling Pitch:** Demonstrate you have actually listened to their show and offer a specific, tailored, and valuable topic you are uniquely qualified to discuss, filling a gap in their content.
    - **Prepare and Deliver:** Ensure high-quality audio recording, prepare key talking points, and naturally mention your podcast and its key differentiators during the interview. *Provide a clear, easy-to-remember URL/CTA.*
- **Cross-Promotion Strategies:**
    - **Swap-Outs:** Mutually promote each other's shows (and specific episodes) in your respective feeds via mid-roll or end-roll promos, usually for a set number of episodes or downloads.
    - **Joint Episodes (Host Swap):** Collaborate on a single episode where each host interviews the other, or they co-

host a discussion on a shared topic to expose both audiences to new content seamlessly.

- ◦ **Feed Drops:** Temporarily adding another highly aligned podcast's full episode to your feed (and vice versa) for a massive, but short-lived, burst of visibility for both parties. This is typically reserved for major partnerships or launches.

Phase IV: The Feedback Loop: Leveraging Analytics for Optimization and Iteration

Marketing is a scientific process requiring constant calibration, not guesswork. Regularly review analytics from your hosting platform, website, and promotional channels. This feedback loop is the difference between a static presence and dynamic growth.

- **Downloads and Listener Demographics:** Understand *what* content is resonating (high-performing episodes) and *who* is listening (confirming/refining the persona). Track where listeners drop off to inform content pacing.
- **Episode Performance:** Pinpoint which episodes attract the most downloads or new subscriptions, providing empirical data for future content ideation and topic selection. Look for patterns in length, guest, and topic.
- **Marketing Campaign Effectiveness:** Track which social media posts, advertising campaigns, guest appearances, or email campaigns correlate with the biggest surge in downloads or new subscriptions. **Use UTM parameters** (unique tracking codes on links) for maximum tracking accuracy across all paid and owned media channels.
- **Monetization Metrics:** Track conversion rates for affiliate links or specific sponsor offers to provide data-backed reports to potential and current advertisers.

Analytics provide the crucial, non-negotiable feedback to refine your content strategy and optimize your marketing efforts, transforming your podcast from an abstract idea into a widely discovered, deeply engaged, and cherished resource. The true dynamic imperative is the commitment to this continuous cycle of strategy, execution, measurement, and optimization.

13

Monetization Strategies for Podcasters

The transformation of a passion for audio content into a financially sustainable podcast is a complex and demanding journey that requires a strategic, multi-faceted approach to revenue generation. As a podcast accumulates influence, measurable downloads, and, most importantly, a deeply dedicated community, embracing and expertly executing diverse monetization models becomes absolutely crucial for long-term viability and growth. This disciplined process effectively elevates content creation from a personal hobby into a thriving, professional business entity. The contemporary monetization landscape is vibrant, characterized by its constant evolution and the proliferation of sophisticated strategies that must be precisely tailored to the specific nature of the content, the size and detailed demographics of the audience, and the overarching financial goals of the creators. Ultimate, enduring success in this domain fundamentally hinges upon clearly defining the inherent, unique value proposition of the podcast and accurately understanding the audience's proven willingness to invest in or financially support the work they consume and cherish.

1. Advertising and Sponsorships (The Bedrock of Ad-Supported Podcasting)

Advertising remains the historical bedrock and most widely established model for podcast monetization. This strategy revolves around the systematic sale of designated advertising slots strategically placed within the audio episodes, converting listenership into quantifiable impressions.

Detailed Ad Formats and Strategic Placement:

- **Pre-roll:** These are brief, impactful advertisements, typically spanning 15 to 30 seconds, positioned right at the functional beginning of an episode, often before the main content or introduction jingle. They guarantee high visibility and broad reach, though creators must be aware that savvy listeners often have the habit of skipping them using in-app fast-forward controls.
- **Mid-roll:** These represent the longest and often most detailed advertisements, ranging robustly from 60 to 90 seconds, and are carefully inserted during organic, natural breaks in the content (e.g., between segments, topic changes, or chapters). They consistently prove to be the most effective format in terms of conversion and recall due to their less intrusive placement and the sufficient time allowance for a comprehensive brand message or detailed product explanation.
- **Post-roll:** Short ads, again 15 to 30 seconds in length, strategically placed at the very conclusion of an episode, following the primary content and closing remarks. They are typically reserved for softer calls to action, gentle brand reminders, cross-promotions for the podcaster's own projects, or simple thank-yous to the sponsors.

Advanced Ad Delivery Mechanisms: Maximizing Revenue and Targeting:

- **Dynamic Ad Insertion (DAI):** This is a technological powerhouse where advertisements are programmatically inserted into the audio feed *at the precise moment a listener downloads or streams an episode*. This allows for sophisticated audience targeting (by geography, device, time of day, or specific demographic data), unparalleled flexibility for advertisers, and the critical ability to update or swap out advertisements even in older, archived episodes. DAI is recognized as the most practical, efficient, and scalable solution for podcasts focused on maximizing ad revenue as they grow their back catalog.
- **"Baked-in" Ads:** These are advertisements that are permanently recorded, mixed, and embedded directly into the audio track during the initial editing and production phase. While they offer less flexibility for campaign changes or targeting, they are often favored for high-value direct sponsorship reads, as they ensure a seamless, permanent, and lasting integration into the content, which some brands value for host-read authenticity.

Understanding Revenue Models: Pricing the Listenership:

- **Cost Per Mille (CPM):** The prevailing industry standard where the advertiser agrees to pay a predefined rate (e.g., $15.00–$30.00, though rates vary significantly by niche and audience quality) for every one thousand downloads, which equates to one thousand ad impressions. This model is best suited for achieving broad brand awareness, scaling campaigns, and maximizing overall reach.
- **Cost Per Acquisition (CPA):** A highly performance-based model where the podcaster earns a measurable commission solely for each specific listener action successfully completed via a

unique promo code or dedicated tracking link (e.g., a direct purchase, a newsletter sign-up, or a free trial activation). This is the ideal model for direct response sales and measurable conversions, often utilized by e-commerce or subscription box companies.

Securing and Managing Direct Sponsorships: The Professional Approach:

1. **Strategic Brand Identification and Vetting:** The first critical step is to meticulously select potential partners whose products, services, and core corporate values demonstrate an authentic, non-negotiable, and deep alignment with the podcast's specific niche and the core demographics of its audience. This ensures the recommendation is genuine and trustworthy.
2. **Creation of a Professional Media Kit:** This is the podcast's professional sales brochure and primary marketing tool. It must be comprehensive, including a detailed podcast overview, granular audience demographics (age, location, interests, income), verified download statistics (certified by an IAB-compliant host), evidence of listener engagement, a clear articulation of advertising offerings and corresponding rate card, and full contact information.
3. **Customized Pitch Development:** The outreach should never be generic. It must precisely explain *how* the podcast's unique, engaged audience and platform can directly help the prospective brand achieve its specific marketing objectives, with a strong, data-driven focus on audience alignment and the host's influence.
4. **Host-Read Ads and Authenticity:** The host, leveraging the established trust they have built with their audience over time, delivers the advertisement. The read should be natural, conversational, and authentic, blending seamlessly with the show's tone, and must always conclude with a distinct, clear, and easy-to-re-

member call to action (e.g., "To get 10% off your first order, use code PODCAST at checkout").

5. **Unwavering Transparency and Disclosure:** It is both an essential ethical best practice and often a strict legal requirement (e.g., FTC guidelines in the US) to clearly and audibly inform the audience that a segment is a paid advertisement or sponsorship (e.g., "This episode is brought to you by..." or "A word from our sponsor..."). This preserves the listener-creator trust.

2. Direct Listener Support and Membership (Cultivating Community Investment)

This model represents a powerful capitalization on deep audience loyalty, effectively transforming passive listeners into active, invested financial stakeholders in the show's ongoing production. It is highly valued across the industry for offering one of the most stable, predictable, and authentic revenue streams available, as it is decoupled from volatile ad markets.

Leveraging Membership Platforms (e.g., Patreon, Substack, Memberful, Supercast):

Membership platforms facilitate recurring financial commitments, typically billed monthly, in exchange for a predefined set of exclusive benefits and access.

- **Tiered Structure Implementation:** Design several distinct support levels (e.g., bronze, silver, gold) each with incrementally increasing rewards, to effectively accommodate different listener budgets and commitment levels (e.g., $3/month for basic bonus content, $10/month for all perks plus Discord access, $50/month for a personal shout-out and annual merchandise).

- **Creating Compelling Perks: Defining the Value Exchange:** The rewards offered must provide tangible, highly desirable value to the patrons, ensuring the recurring financial commitment is convincingly justified:
    - **Bonus Episodes/Series:** Exclusive, non-public content like extended interviews, listener Q&A sessions, one-off mini-series, or deep-dive analyses on related topics.
    - **Early Access:** Offering regular public episodes a full day or two before the public release date.
    - **Ad-Free Versions:** Providing a premium, uninterrupted listening experience for all episodes.
    - **Exclusive Merchandise/Discounts:** Access to unique, patrons-only physical goods or a percentage off the main public merch store.
    - **Private Community Access:** Granting entry to an exclusive digital space (e.g., a dedicated private Discord channel, Slack workspace, or private Facebook Group) to foster direct creator-listener interaction and build a sense of belonging.
    - **Behind-the-Scenes Content:** Sharing production bloopers, creator commentaries on episodes, or insights into the show's planning and production process.

Simplified One-Time Donations:

Platforms like Buy Me a Coffee, Ko-fi, or PayPal offer a much simpler, low-friction avenue for listeners to provide a one-time, non-recurring gesture of appreciation or "tip" for a specific episode they particularly enjoyed. This serves as an excellent entry point for non-committal support.

Keys to Long-Term Success with Listener Support:

- **Foster a Community Ecosystem:** The revenue generated is a byproduct of the relationship. Nurture and actively engage with patrons through consistent interaction, recognizing their contribution by name, and asking for their input on future content.
- **Radical Transparency:** Explicitly communicate to the audience precisely and emotionally how their financial support is being utilized (e.g., "Your support funds better editing software and transcription services," or "We're saving up for new professional microphones to improve sound quality").
- **Clear and Natural Call-to-Action (CTA):** Regularly, but organically and without sounding overly demanding or transactional, remind the audience of the available support mechanisms. Weave the CTA into the natural flow of the show, often at the end of the episode.

3. Affiliate Marketing (The Performance-Driven Strategy)

Affiliate marketing is a purely performance-based monetization strategy where the podcaster earns a defined commission for every successful sale or qualified lead successfully generated through a unique tracking link or promotional code they share with their audience.

- **Program Selection Strategy:** Only partner with reputable companies whose products or services are highly relevant, authentic, and genuinely useful to the podcast's content and the audience's stated interests. Authenticity is the ultimate currency; a mismatch can damage listener trust.
- **Seamless Content Integration:** The product recommendations must be woven naturally and conversationally into the regular flow of the content, sounding like a genuine, trusted personal endorsement from the host rather than a blatant, scripted sales pitch.

- **Dedicated Promotional Content:** Consider strategically creating entire episodes dedicated to reviewing, exploring, or demonstrating a specific product or service in-depth, organically including the affiliate information as a natural part of the review process.
- **The Critical Role of Show Notes:** Since a listener cannot click on an audio file, the show notes serve as the primary, essential gateway to the commission. They must include clear, easily identifiable affiliate links and memorable, easy-to-type discount codes (e.g., "Link in the show notes at [podcastwebsite.com]").
- **Mandatory Disclosure:** Always maintain absolute transparency about the affiliate relationship. This builds essential, long-term trust with the audience and is a non-negotiable legal requirement (e.g., "Note: As an Amazon Associate, I earn from qualifying purchases at no extra cost to you.").
- **Tracking and Optimization:** Utilize unique, customized links or codes for different campaigns, episodes, or ad placements to accurately track which promotional methods and which specific products are most effective, allowing for continuous optimization and focus on high-converting offers.

4. Premium Content and Paid Subscriptions (The Exclusive Experience)

This highly leveraged model involves offering an exclusive or substantially enhanced listening experience directly to a self-selected, paying subscriber base via dedicated, often in-app, distribution channels.

- **Exclusive Content Series:** The creation of entirely separate, high-value premium podcasts, distinct narrative series, or intensive deep-dive analyses that are accessible only behind a defined paywall. This content should not feel like leftovers but rather a dedicated, premium product.

- **Enhanced Episode Experience:** Offering premium versions of the regular, public episodes. This most often takes the form of ad-free listening, extended-length interviews with guests, or the inclusion of exclusive bonus segments appended to the core content.
- **Subscription Platform Utilization:** Leverage seamless, in-app access platforms such as Apple Podcasts Subscriptions, Spotify's subscription tools, or third-party premium content hosts (like Supercast) for frictionless user experience and easy payment processing.
- **Unassailable Value Proposition:** For a subscription to succeed, the premium content *must* be demonstrably valuable, clearly distinct from the free offering, and highly desirable enough to convincingly justify the recurring cost to the consumer. The content must solve a problem, entertain uniquely, or provide exclusive access.

5. Leveraging Brand and Expertise (Monetizing Authority)

This strategy focuses on monetizing the authority, credibility, and deep connection the podcast has established with its audience by creating and selling tangible products, specialized services, and intellectual property.

- **Branded Merchandise:** Selling physical items (e.g., custom-designed t-shirts, coffee mugs, stickers, hats) that strongly align with the podcast's unique identity, internal jokes, specific catchphrases, or visual brand.

  - **Dual Benefits:** Merch is a direct, profitable revenue stream and simultaneously acts as powerful, organic marketing as listeners effectively become mobile brand ambassadors for the show when they wear or use the items.
  - **Fulfillment Options:** Utilize print-on-demand (POD) services (e.g., Printful, Teespring, Redbubble) to minimize upfront inventory costs, manage logistics, and eliminate warehousing issues, or opt for wholesale suppliers for greater cost efficiency and control at higher sales volumes.
- **Online Courses and Digital Products:** The podcast's core expertise is packaged into structured, actionable learning materials (e.g., premium e-books, self-paced masterclasses, intensive downloadable workshops, or specialized templates).

  - **Development Process:** Identify a specific, highly actionable learning outcome that the audience frequently asks about. Structure the content into engaging, logical modules. Use specialized platforms like Teachable, Kajabi, or Thinkific to professionally host, market, and securely sell the courses.
  - **Podcast as Lead Generation:** The podcast itself transforms into an incredibly powerful top-of-funnel marketing channel, attracting and pre-qualifying students who are eager for the deeper, specialized knowledge being offered by the host/expert.
- **Professional Services and Events:** Offering direct, high-touch, personalized engagement and support that commands a premium price.

  - **Coaching/Consulting:** Working one-on-one or in small groups with clients, leveraging the specific expertise and thought leadership demonstrated consistently on the podcast to help them solve their unique problems.

- **Live Events/Workshops:** Hosting ticketed, in-person or virtual live recordings, comprehensive Q&A sessions, or intensive, high-value workshops, allowing for community interaction and direct ticket revenue. This is also a strong way to gather testimonials.
- **Paid Speaking Engagements:** Monetizing the host's credibility as a recognized thought leader by actively securing paid speaking opportunities at major industry conferences, corporate events, academic forums, or trade shows.

The Indispensable Power of Revenue Diversification

Relying on any single source of income—be it advertising, listener patronage, or course sales—leaves the podcast financially vulnerable to unpredictable market fluctuations, sudden platform changes (e.g., a host raises its fees), or sharp shifts in audience behavior. The most financially successful and resilient podcasts invariably adopt a deliberate multi-pronged approach, strategically combining several monetization models. For instance, a show might simultaneously use **Dynamic Ad Insertion (DAI)** for a broad-based scalable revenue stream, cultivate a dedicated **Patreon** community for its most loyal fans to ensure a stable base income, and periodically launch an **Online Course** to monetize its core expertise through high-value sales cycles. Continuous experimentation, rigorous performance analysis (tracking which methods yield the highest return), and proactive adaptation are the fundamental keys to discovering the optimal, protective blend of strategies that can reliably support sustainable growth, ensuring both financial stability and the creative freedom necessary to produce truly exceptional, uncompromising content.

14

Analytics, Growth Tracking, and AI Insights

The journey of a podcast from a spontaneous, heartfelt venture to a robust, profitable, and influential media platform is no longer paved by chance. It is a carefully engineered trajectory, mandating a shift from anecdotal decision-making to a rigorous, **data-driven methodology**. This systematic approach requires the not only the diligent harvesting of performance metrics from hosting platforms and directories but, crucially, their alchemical transformation. By applying the analytical power of artificial intelligence (AI), raw statistical data is converted into a dynamic, **predictive blueprint** for continuous content excellence, accelerated audience acquisition, and sustainable growth.-----I. Foundational Podcasting Metrics: The "What" – Granular Audience Measurement and Behavior

The bedrock of any effective podcast strategy is the establishment of accurate, defensible metrics related to audience reach and consumption habits. These core data points define the current state and serve as the necessary baseline for all subsequent analytical and strategic endeavors.

- **Downloads and Requests: Decoding Consumption Intent**
  While "download" remains the ubiquitous metric, its definition has evolved. It signifies the *potential* for a listen—the request for

the episode file by a listener's device. Modern, sophisticated analytics now apply stringent filters to exclude bot-driven activity, incomplete file transfers, and duplicate requests, yielding a far more trustworthy metric: **Total Unique Downloads**. The strategic significance of this number is not its absolute magnitude, but the **velocity and trend analysis**.

  - **Strategic Interpretation:** A rapid, high spike in the initial 48-72 hours confirms powerful initial appeal (often driven by pre-promotion or subscriber anticipation). Conversely, a sustained, long-tail download pattern extending weeks or months is the signature of **evergreen content value**, indicating episodes that function as perpetual audience entry points.

- **Unique Listeners (The True Audience Count): Gauging Genuine Reach**
This metric provides a **superior measure of actual reach** by representing the number of distinct, identified individuals who have consumed at least a minimum threshold of your content within a specified analysis window (e.g., weekly or monthly). Hosting services leverage heuristics—such as IP addresses, device identifiers, and platform-specific user IDs—to meticulously filter repeat downloads by the same user.

  - **Advanced Strategic Interpretation:** The **ratio of Total Downloads to Unique Listeners** is a vital diagnostic tool. A consistently **high ratio** suggests a smaller, intensely loyal, and likely *binge-listening* core audience that frequently revisits or shares content. Conversely, a **low ratio** signals broad but potentially shallow reach, demanding an immediate strategic pivot toward deeper retention and loyalty-building efforts.

- **Listener Retention and Drop-off Analysis: The Stethoscope of Content Quality**
Arguably the single most critical metric, retention is measured as the average percentage of an episode consumed. The resulting **retention graph** is the podcaster's stethoscope, providing an X-ray view of the episode's structural health and pacing effectiveness.

    - **Deep Dive Diagnostic:** Precisely located, sharp drops invariably pinpoint specific failure points within the content timeline. These may include a poorly integrated or overly aggressive **Call-to-Action (CTA)**, excessive or poorly placed advertising, a disruptive technical audio flaw, or an unduly protracted, uninteresting introductory segment. Key failure points to monitor include the **"5-minute cliff"** (where casual listeners often decide to commit or abandon) and the **"mid-episode slump,"** both of which necessitate surgical content improvements focused on pacing, hook placement, and payoff structure.
- **Geographic, Device, and Platform Segmentation: Informing Optimization and Commerce**
Detailed demographic and technical data informs both content localization and effective monetization strategies.

    - **Geographic Data:** This informs the localization of cultural references, the optimal timing of episode releases to align with regional peak listening hours, and alignment with specific international events. It is also crucial for guiding the strategic placement of geographically-targeted advertisements and sponsorships.
    - **Device and Platform Data:** This is essential for technical optimization (e.g., prioritizing mono compatibility and accessibility if a high percentage of the audience uses smart speakers or budget earbuds) and for focusing promo-

tional spend. If 80% of listeners are identified on a single platform (e.g., Spotify), promotional efforts must be heavily skewed toward leveraging that platform's specific algorithms, features, and native ad formats.

-----II. Interpreting the Data: The "Why" and "How" – Establishing the Strategic Narrative

The true leap in strategic podcasting occurs when metrics are no longer merely reported, but **woven into a coherent, actionable narrative**. This step transforms the *what* (the data) into the *why* (the insight) and explicitly dictates the *how* (the future production changes).

- **Comparative Episode Performance Analysis: Isolating the Variables of Success**
  A mandatory, rigorous analysis involves the comparison of **Top-Performing Episodes** (those with both high unique listeners and superior retention) and **Under-Performing Episodes** (those with low engagement). The primary objective is to scientifically isolate and define the variables consistently linked to success.

  - *Success Variables Identification:* Was the topic exceptionally timely or evergreen? Did a high-profile guest draw in a new audience segment? Was there a successful experimental format (e.g., a solo deep dive versus a traditional interview)?
  - *Failure Patterns Diagnosis:* Was the audio quality substandard? Did a misleading title or show notes create a **promise-delivery gap**? Was the content deemed too abstract, overly dense, or lacking a clear takeaway? This focused comparison drives precise, evidence-based adjustments to the content development pipeline.

- **Topic Analysis and Depth of Engagement: Distinguishing Interest from Dedication**
  While high download numbers reflect *initial interest*, average listening time and the retention graph reflect *true, sustained engagement*. Analyzing retention against the episode's core topic yields the most nuanced insight into audience appetite.

  - **Nuanced Example:** A hyper-niche, highly complex topic may predictably result in fewer total downloads, yet exhibit near 100% retention. This signals a deeply dedicated, valuable, and highly monetizable subgroup. Conversely, a broadly popular topic with unexpectedly low retention suggests superficial interest or a failure to deliver on the initial promise, necessitating a structural re-think of the episode's core thesis and pacing.
- **Trend and Correlation Analysis for Acquisition: Proving Channel Effectiveness**
  Monitoring the macro-level health of the podcast (e.g., sustained growth versus volatile spikes) is continuous. Critical analysis involves systematically correlating specific external marketing actions with internal metric performance.

  - *Key Correlation Test:* Did the host's recent guest appearance on a major complementary show (the external action) lead to a significant, sustained spike in **new unique listeners** and a measurable increase in **subscriber growth**? If the correlation is strong, the strategy is validated, and similar guesting opportunities must be heavily prioritized in the content calendar. This process effectively proves the Return on Investment (ROI) of specific acquisition channels.
- **Mapping the Listener's Journey and Onboarding: Optimizing the Content Funnel**

Understanding the consumption pattern of a new listener is crucial to optimizing the content onboarding process. If a new unique listener consistently *skips* the latest episode to immediately binge on a specific "evergreen" episode (e.g., "Episode 1: The Foundations"), that evergreen content must be made exponentially more prominent as the official, friction-free "start here" recommendation. Tracking the time it takes for a new unique listener to convert into a full-fledged subscriber informs the **optimal onboarding sequence** and content funnel design.

- **Synthesizing Quantitative and Qualitative Data: The Holistic View**
  Quantitative metrics (the numbers) answer *how many* and *how much*; qualitative feedback (reviews, social media comments, listener emails, direct feedback) answers the indispensable *why*. A sudden, minor dip in retention might only be explained by a recurring qualitative comment complaining about a specific, subtle aspect—for instance, "The background music bed was too loud during the interview segment." Conversely, overwhelmingly positive qualitative feedback about a new, experimental segment instantly validates its continuation and expansion into a recurring format.

-----III. The AI Advantage: The "What Next" – Predictive and Nuanced Insight Generation

Artificial Intelligence represents the modern evolution of analytics, fundamentally transcending historical reporting. AI introduces robust **predictive power** and is capable of extracting complex correlations far too subtle and multivariate for standard human analysis. AI transforms the strategic roadmap from being fundamentally reactive to decisively **proactive**.

- **Advanced Sentiment Analysis (via NLP): Granular Feedback Extraction**
  AI-powered Natural Language Processing (NLP) is deployed to sift through the immense, unstructured text data found in reviews, comments, social media mentions, and listener emails. It moves light-years beyond simple positive/negative categorization to identify **granular, feature-specific sentiment** tied to exact timestamps in the episode.

  - *Actionable AI Insight:* Instead of a vague conclusion like "Listeners generally like the show," the AI reports: "85% of comments praised the host's clear structure in the first segment, but sentiment dropped by a significant 22% during the call-to-action segment at the 42:15 mark due to perceived aggressive tone and repetitive language." This instantly pinpoints *exactly* where and how to refine the script and delivery for future episodes.
- **Predictive Listener Trend Forecasting: Establishing Thought Leadership**
  Sophisticated AI engines analyze the podcast's internal historical performance data alongside external, macro-level market signals—including global search engine trend velocity, competitor content release schedules, and the direction of trending discussions in related social media niches. This allows the system to accurately **forecast the likely peak success of future content themes**.

  - *Proactive Strategy:* Instead of merely reacting to a topic that has already peaked, the AI forecasts that "The intersection of Topic A (e.g., Quantum Computing) and Topic B (e.g., Ethical Supply Chains) will peak in listener interest and search volume in precisely four weeks." This grants the production team the crucial lead time to proactively develop and release content that perfectly aligns with peak demand, establishing the show as a timely and authoritative thought leader.

- **Intricate Pattern Recognition and Micro-Correlations: Maximizing Monetization**
AI is uniquely capable of identifying complex, multivariate correlations that are either invisible or appear nonsensical within standard, siloed human analysis.

    - *Hyper-Specific Targeting Example:* AI discovers the pattern: "Listeners who download on Tuesdays between 6 PM and 8 PM via an Apple Watch device, and who listen past the 75% mark, are 40% more likely to click on a specific category of affiliate link (e.g., productivity software) than the general audience." This non-obvious insight allows for hyper-specific, dynamic ad insertion and call-to-action targeting, dramatically maximizing monetization efficiency and conversion rates.

- **Sophisticated Audience Segmentation and Dynamic Personas: Boosting Loyalty**
AI utilizes deep behavioral data (not merely static demographics) to create detailed, continuously evolving listener personas.

    - *AI-Derived Personas:* Examples include "The Binge Listener" (defined by high back-catalogue consumption), "The Topic Specialist" (who exclusively listens to episodes on specific, narrow themes), and "The Early Adopter" (defined by listening only in the first 24 hours post-release). This segmentation allows for highly personalized and segmented email marketing, targeted platform advertising, and tailored community-fostering strategies, significantly boosting both listener satisfaction and long-term loyalty.

-----IV. Establishing and Tracking Strategic Growth Goals: The SMART Framework for Accountability

For growth to be sustainable, measurable, and intentional, it must be anchored by the **SMART** framework: Specific, Measurable, Achievable, Relevant, and Time-bound goals. This framework ensures laser focus, resource accountability, and a clear path to execution.

- **Defining Clear and Tiered Goals:**
    - **Short-Term (3-12 Months):** These goals are highly tactical, focused on measurable inputs or immediate outputs. Examples: Increase average Unique Downloads by 15% in the next 90 days; demonstrably improve listener retention past the critical 15-minute mark by 5 percentage points (as informed by AI analysis); secure a specific number (Z) of positive, qualitative reviews on a key distribution platform.
    - **Long-Term (1-3+ Years):** These goals are strategic, focused on establishing enduring market position, brand authority, and financial sustainability. Examples: Achieve a volume of X monthly unique downloads necessary to reach the top 5% of all podcasts in the chosen category; establish the podcast as the clear, leading voice in the industry niche; achieve a specified monthly monetization level required to fully sustain and expand production quality.
- **Key Metrics for Continuous Strategic Tracking:** A focused, easily digestible performance dashboard is essential to prevent "analysis paralysis."
    - **Reach & Growth: Unique Downloads** and **Subscriber Growth** (The Core Measures of Audience Size and Loyalty).

- **Engagement & Quality: Listener Retention** and **Drop-off Rates** (The Core Measures of Content Quality and Pacing).
- **Action & Community: Engagement Metrics** (Social Shares, Website/Newsletter Sign-ups Driven by Podcast CTAs).
- **Sustainability: Monetization Metrics** (Affiliate Link Conversion Rates, Sponsorship Revenue/Value Per 1,000 Downloads).

- **The Iterative, Adaptive Process: Strategy as a Cycle**

Strategic planning is inherently a continuous cycle, not a static, fixed document. Mandatory weekly or monthly "analytics reviews" must rigorously compare current performance against the defined SMART goals. The **willingness to immediately pivot** based on evidence is critical: If a new, experimental interview format yields significantly lower retention, the strategy must be instantly adjusted or abandoned. AI-powered insights—such as "a 5-minute reduction in intro music and the removal of the mid-roll ad will likely increase retention by 3%"—guide precise, data-backed course correction with the highest probability of success.

- **Holistic Data Integration (The 360-Degree View): Beyond the Host**

A truly effective strategic roadmap demands the rigorous integration of data streams that extend well beyond the core hosting platform's metrics. This integration is crucial for understanding the complete listener lifecycle.

- **Website Analytics:** Tracking listener behavior *after* they click a link in the show notes (e.g., time on page, purchase conversions, lead magnet downloads).
- **Social Media Analytics:** Tracking precisely which platforms, post formats, and messaging types drive the

highest quality traffic (defined as new unique listeners with high retention).

- **Email Marketing Platform Analytics:** Tracking subscriber conversion rates and comparing the depth of engagement of the email audience versus the general listening audience, proving the value of the lead capture strategy.

By fully embracing this integrated, adaptive, strategically focused, and AI-augmented approach, a podcast can decisively graduate from simply existing as a hobby to becoming a thriving, influential, and financially viable media asset that consistently delivers content that resonates deeply with a dedicated, eagerly anticipating, and ever-growing global audience.

15

The Future of Podcasting with Evolving AI

The future of podcasting is not merely changing; it is being fundamentally and rapidly reshaped by the transformative capabilities of Artificial Intelligence. This evolution pushes AI past the role of a simple utility, establishing it as a profound co-creator, hyper-personalized content orchestrator, and an essential partner in community building and audience connection. For content creators, this monumental shift demands the immediate adoption of an agile, innovative, and deeply ethically conscious mindset, which will be the prerequisite for those who aim to not only survive but truly thrive in the coming audio landscape.

I. AI as the Co-Creator and Innovation Catalyst

The functional expansion of AI is moving beyond basic operational assistance to sophisticated co-creation, dramatically pushing the boundaries of what is possible in audio storytelling and production. This partnership fundamentally alters the creative workflow, injecting unprecedented levels of efficiency and complexity.

- **Complex Narrative Generation and World-Building:** Future AI systems will transcend basic script generation to deeply internalize and expertly apply principles of dramatic structure, sophisticated pacing, thematic development, and deep character motivation. It will gain the capacity to generate entire, cohesive fictional series, expertly weave together multiple complex storylines across seasons, and maintain distinct, consistent emotional and psychological arcs for a large and diverse cast of characters. This advanced capability will democratize sophisticated audio drama production, significantly lowering the technical and resource barrier to entry for ambitious narrative projects that previously required large teams.

- **Nuanced Dialogue, Subtext, and Indistinguishable Performance:** AI is poised to create dialogue that is not only grammatically correct but profoundly realistic, emotionally resonant, and rich with subtle subtext that accurately reflects a character's deep personality, immediate context, and complex relationships. In both fictional and non-fictional formats, this linguistic precision will elevate authenticity and immediacy. Critically, AI voice synthesis will reach a point where it can mimic a virtually limitless range of vocal inflections, regional accents, subtle emotional tones (e.g., sarcasm, hesitation, confidence), and diverse performance styles, leading to AI-voiced performances that are utterly indistinguishable from human talent. This enables hyper-personalized voice selection for individual listeners, transforming their subjective listening experience into something uniquely tailored.
- **Novel, Dynamic, and Adaptive Podcast Formats:** A key dimension of AI's potential lies in its ability to generate formats that are inherently dynamic, non-linear, and adapt in real-time to user input or contextual changes.

    - **Exploratory/Choose-Your-Own-Adventure Narratives:** The narrative paths of a story will shift dynamically based on real-time listener engagement data, expressed curiosity via integrated voice commands, or explicit choices made by the listener. This creates a highly personal, interactive, and non-linear consumption experience with significant replay value.

  - **Conversational Learning Experiences:** AI can simulate a highly effective, personalized one-on-one tutoring session. It adapts its teaching style, the complexity of the material, the pace of delivery, and the depth of explanation to the individual learner's expressed knowledge level, rate of comprehension, and even preferred learning style. This fundamentally transforms passive listening into a highly active, measurable, and effective educational experience.

- **Collaborative Partnership and Synthetic Expertise:** AI will evolve from a tool into a highly sophisticated brainstorming and objective creative partner. It can offer objective, data-driven feedback on concept viability (e.g., predicting audience resonance) and instantaneously generate a multitude of alternative creative possibilities from a single initial idea, drastically accelerating and optimizing the entire pre-production timeline. Furthermore, AI can create and conduct highly detailed "synthetic" expert interviews, democratizing access to deep, specialized knowledge in niche fields without the logistical and financial challenges of securing human experts.

II. The Era of Hyper-Personalization: One-to-One Audio

AI is fundamentally shattering the traditional broadcast model, which pushed the same content to all listeners, ushering in an era of deeply intimate, one-to-one audio dialogue through radical hyper-personalization. The podcast becomes a service designed for a single user.

- **Dynamic Content Assembly and Semantic Curation:** The future podcast feed will not be a static playlist of episodes.

AI will curate, remix, and dynamically assemble a vast library of granular audio segments—potentially sourced from hundreds of episodes, specialized knowledge bases, or real-time news feeds—synthesizing this information into a coherent, flowing narrative. This content will be precisely tailored not just to a listener's broad interests, but to their specific, nuanced current search queries, their dynamically measured existing knowledge level on a subject, and the context of their immediate needs.

- **Contextual Awareness and Physiological Adaptation:** Personalization will extend far beyond stated interests to incorporate the listener's immediate, real-world context. This includes the time of day, current geographical location, detected mood (analyzed through voice input, listening history, or interaction patterns), and even real-time physiological state monitored via wearable devices (e.g., heart rate, stress levels, physical activity). An AI could instantaneously pivot from a complex, cognitively demanding deep-dive lecture to a calming soundscape, guided meditation, or motivational content if it detects significant signs of listener stress, distraction, or mental fatigue.
- **Enhanced Loyalty and Exponential Engagement:** This highly tailored, instantaneous, and optimized approach ensures that every listening session feels uniquely relevant, directly optimized for the individual's needs, and perfectly calibrated to their current state. The result is a profound increase in listener loyalty, a reduced skip rate, and significantly longer, more consistent engagement times, maximizing the value of every minute of audio.
- **Bespoke Episode Generation on Demand:** Instead of the creator producing a single, monolithic episode, AI will be capable of generating multiple, thematically divergent versions of the same core content instantly. For example, an episode covering a historical event might have versions that focus purely on the military strategy, the social and cultural impact, the economic consequences, or the key biographies, ensuring maximum resonance

with distinct segments of the audience based on their individual listener profiles and stated preferences.

III. Fostering Community and Engagement at Scale

AI offers powerful, scalable tools designed to cultivate and deepen the relationship between podcasters and their audience, turning passive consumers into active, engaged contributors, and managing community dynamics effectively.

- **Intelligent Listener Support and Knowledge Bases:** Highly advanced, AI-powered chatbots and voice agents will provide instant, accurate, and contextually aware answers to listener follow-up questions, inquiries, and requests for deeper resources and links. This capability frees up human creators from repetitive, high-volume Q&A while significantly enhancing the audience's comprehension, sense of immediate access, and post-listening engagement.
- **Real-Time Community and Sentiment Management:** AI systems can continuously monitor online forums, Discord servers, social media platforms, and comment sections for rapid shifts in collective sentiment. They can identify emerging subtopics of discussion, flag potentially inappropriate or toxic content instantly, and alert community managers to points of confusion, urgent trends, or high-value feedback. This enables proactive content refinement, highly effective community facilitation, and the rapid de-escalation of conflicts.
- **Interactive and Dynamic Episodes:** AI can manage and scale listener interactions in ways previously impossible for a human production team. It can categorize, filter, and summarize thousands of submitted questions to identify and prioritize recurring themes for "Q&A" segments, generate on-the-fly trivia

based on recent content, or even incorporate listener-generated choices (e.g., poll/voting results) directly into a narrative or instructional path. This fundamentally fosters a dynamic sense of co-creation and shared ownership.

- **Personalized Outreach and Fan Identification:** By analyzing granular engagement patterns, including completion rates, specific segment skips and replays, and external interaction data (e.g., website visits), AI can help podcasters accurately identify their most loyal, influential, or niche-interested fans. This deep understanding enables the delivery of highly targeted communications, personalized thank-you messages, and early-access content, ensuring new material resonates deeply with specific, active sub-interests within the overall audience, optimizing marketing spend.

IV. Ethical Imperatives for the AI Future

The immense and rapidly growing power of AI necessitates a rigorous, proactive examination of ethical frameworks to ensure the integrity, trustworthiness, sustainability, and fairness of the podcasting medium and the creative economy it supports.

- **Authenticity, Disclosure, and Misinformation Combat:** The potential for sophisticated AI-generated deepfakes and the rapid, convincing spread of misinformation is a critical societal and industry concern. Establishing universal digital watermarking, employing robust authentication technologies, and mandating clear, standardized labeling policies (e.g., "This episode utilizes AI-generated dialogue" or "This voice is synthetic and licensed") are essential to maintaining public credibility and clearly distinguishing human-created from AI-generated or manipulated content.

- **Intellectual Property, Licensing, and Fair Compensation:** New legal, ethical, and creative frameworks must be immediately established to definitively clarify ownership, copyright, and licensing for content that is both AI-assisted and fully AI-generated. A clear, equitable system must protect the livelihoods of human creators and ensure fair compensation, particularly when unique human voices, distinctive personas, or established creative styles are replicated, trained upon, or licensed by an AI model.
- **Algorithmic Bias and Countering Filter Bubbles:** AI systems must be intentionally designed with robust guardrails to actively encourage listener exposure to diverse viewpoints, counter established assumptions, and prevent listeners from becoming isolated in self-reinforcing "echo chambers" created by over-personalization. Ensuring fairness, equity, and broad accessibility in the distribution and use of AI creation tools is also paramount to prevent the centralization of creative power.
- **Transparency and Auditable Trust:** Listeners have a fundamental and non-negotiable right to know when they are interacting with an artificial intelligence, whether it is a support chatbot, a synthetic voice narrator, or content that has been significantly edited, restructured, or dynamically generated by an AI algorithm. This level of transparency is the foundation for building and maintaining listener trust and allowing for informed, critical content consumption.
- **Augmentation Over Replacement: The Human-Centric Focus:** Ethical AI development must remain laser-focused on how these tools can strategically augment and exponentially elevate human capabilities and creativity, rather than seeking to displace the creative workforce. AI should be leveraged to automate and handle routine, time-consuming technical, logistical, and analytical tasks, thereby liberating human creators to concentrate

their energy on the most nuanced aspects of storytelling, artistic vision, critical analysis, and emotional connection.

V. Agility and Innovation: The Creator's Mandate

To effectively navigate and shape this dynamic technological landscape, podcasters must cultivate a mindset that is fluid, experimental, and inherently adaptive to continuous, rapid change. The static model of content creation is obsolete.

- **Continuous and Focused Learning:** Creators must make an absolute commitment to stay deeply informed about the rapid proliferation of new AI-powered software applicable to every single stage of production—from ideation and script refinement to advanced audio mastering, dynamic metadata tagging, and granular audience analysis. This knowledge must be prioritized.
- **Experimentation as a Core Tenet:** Dedicated time, budget, and human resources must be proactively carved out to test new AI tools and creative approaches without the immediate pressure of commercial success. Every experiment, even those that appear to be technical failures, must be viewed as valuable data that informs future strategic decisions and process optimization. An 'experimental budget' is essential.
- **Proactive Innovation Mindset:** Podcasters must actively and creatively seek opportunities to push the boundaries of the medium, utilizing AI to explore entirely novel content formats (like the dynamic narrative), analyze granular listener engagement data for immediate feedback loops, and significantly improve production value with optimized time and resource allocation.
- **Rapid Adaptation and Strategic Pivot:** Agility means being prepared to quickly pivot strategies, rapidly repurpose and repackage existing content using new tools, and swiftly integrate

new, effective technologies while ruthlessly discarding ineffective ones in response to market shifts, technological advancements, or audience feedback. This adaptation must always be anchored by the core mission and the established, deep needs of the target audience.

Ultimately, the future of audio content hinges on the profound synergy between human imagination and artificial intelligence. This partnership promises a trajectory where audio content is more diverse, more immediately engaging, more relevant, and more impactful than any format that has preceded it. Podcasters must embrace AI not with apprehension, but as an indispensable, collaborative partner that exponentially amplifies human creativity, transforms the depth of listener connection, and actively shapes the pioneering trajectory of audio storytelling for the next generation.

www.ingramcontent.com/pod-product-compliance
Lightning Source LLC
LaVergne TN
LVHW022227200926
848481LV00006B/2159
* 9 7 9 8 2 9 5 6 0 0 2 4 1 *